ENVIRONMENTAL MAN

ENVIRONMENTAL MAN

WILLIAM KUHNS

Harper & Row, Publishers   *1817*

New York, Evanston, and London

FIRST EDITION

LIBRARY OF CONGRESS CATALOG CARD NUMBER: 69-10472.

To my wife, Elsie

CONTENTS

7

PREFACE

Environmental Man explores the significance of man's contemporary environment for theology. Today's growing awareness of the influence of technology upon man makes it imperative to search out the effects of this environment on the entire range of Christian beliefs and experiences. The book's method is to go after the "interfaces," the bonds between men and particular environments, and base any theological conclusions upon the nature and working of the interfaces. In this way, it can be seen that cars affect the Christian conception of freedom; movies pose enormous challenges to a meaningful liturgy; and modern commodities, with their subtle advertising campaigns, raise serious questions about the meaning of symbols in the Church. Part of whatever future there may be for the Church must lie in its attempt to wrestle with the significance of these environmental factors.

Many thanks to Professor Joseph Sittler of the University of Chicago Divinity School and Dr. Herbert Richardson of St. Michael's College, Toronto, for their sympathetic readings and provocative suggestions. Finally, a grateful appreciation to Mary Ann Rehnke, who typed the manuscript.

WILLIAM KUHNS

ENVIRONMENTAL MAN

1

2001

THE FUTURE OF INTERFACE?

> There's no doubt that we're entering a mechanarchy . . .
> and that our already complex relationship with our machinery
> will become even more complex as the machines become
> more and more intelligent.
>
> Stanley Kubrick*

Many of the great questions of the twentieth century seem
foisted upon us by our technologies—the tools that, even as they
are constantly modifying our lives, we barely understand apart
from the wires and currents which make them work. And what
of the twenty-first century? Will technology become more of a
threat, more of a mystery—or will we come to a truce with its
powers, just as we have been able, in the twentieth century, to
control the social industrial forces so explosive in the nineteenth
century?

Stanley Kubrick's 2001: *A Space Odyssey* is a visual preview
of the upcoming century of space exploration—but even more,
of the meaning of man's interface with his technological environment in that century. As such, it is both a potent example

---

* *Playboy* interview, September, 1968.

of interface and perhaps a guide to the interfaces we will encounter in the future.

Interface is the process initiated by the contact between two systems. Man meets man, man drives a car, man is assaulted by the daily inundation of advertising: these are commonplace interfaces, yet concentrated and influential ones. In all cases the interface is capable of catalyzing a new synergetic level of relationship between the two systems—one, that is, containing more than could be predicted through a separate knowledge of the two systems. So the man driving his car comes to identify himself with the car—not as extension but as completion of himself. In the sudden moment of rage at being sideswiped, a driver does not say, "He hit my car"—but, "He hit me!"

In 2001 interface takes place on a grandiose scale. Indeed man, so suspicious that he was a victim of his environments in the twentieth century, becomes in the twenty-first nothing more than a prop in a dramatic struggle between environments. If the film has any hero, it is space: the stars, planets, and distances that seem to reduce man to proportions he could never really sense on his cloistered planet.

The "story" (or what there is of one) accentuates the film's absorption with future interfaces. The film opens at the birth of man, with two hordes of gorillas fighting over a water hole. A tall, mysterious slab appears; and somehow its appearance acts as a catalyst to the great transition—from ape to weapon-bearing ape, the father of man. Suddenly the film leaps to A.D. 2001 and a spaceship approaching a satellite port. As the ship approaches and enters the port, the audience is caught in the fascination of the ships and the stars themselves. The craft—not man—seem to belong out here, and indeed the spaceport (with its Howard Johnson's restaurant and Hilton Hotel facilities) seems from the inside an extension of the earth, while from the outside it has become a part of the great cosmic movements.

There are the sketchings of a story within the story; another slab has been found on the moon, with radio emissions directed to Jupiter. Soon a gigantic ship resembling two globes linked by a chain of appendixes takes off for Jupiter. Its crew members seem anonymous; its captain is in effect the emotion-programmed computer Hal, who eventually turns against the two waking crew members when they plot against him. Only at this one point in the film—the struggle with Hal—does 2001 reflect the older, traditional forms of interface which dominate drama and film. One man wins out, but only to be mesmerized by blinding psychedelic effects when he reaches the Jupiter atmosphere. He ages rapidly, to become—at his death?—reborn a gestation globe, which has been sent forth in another slab to populate, like the original slab, some other planet with a superhuman species.

In 2001 the interfaces between man and environment, and two environments (the robot and ship, for example; or the ship and the stars), become the center of the drama. There are no conflicts between men, or within men, that engage the viewers; only the conflicts between environments—most notably with outer space and the men and technologies that invade its realms.

Two choice examples are the tension between Dave (one of the two waking crew members on the Jupiter flight) and the computer Hal, and the overall pattern of the film, which suggests that a strategic slab or a trip to Jupiter has a profound, even religious, significance: the ultimate interface.

Dave becomes wary of the smooth-throated computer Hal when Hal seems reluctant to repair a breakdown in communications. The interface, humanized to the point of audience identification of Hal with a human being, concludes in Dave's unscrewing Hal's memory banks—slowly depleting its mind and reducing it from genius to a stuttering mental case. The incident not only plays upon people's incipient fears that computers and robots will turn and defy their masters; it likewise suggests that the technological interface of the future will be as complex, laden with levels of trust and distrust and friendships masking enmities, as the person-to-person interface is today. If men find it hard to live with one another, they may find it yet harder to live with a complex of computers capable of opposing them.

On the scale of the entire film, the interface takes on yet grander dimensions. Theologically the origin and destiny of man have been understood, at least within the Judeo-Christian tradition, as direct works of God, the intervention of the supernatural into the natural. In *2001* the interface between an unseen force on Jupiter and a fortunate tribe of apes decides the birth of man; and eventually, some half a million years later, man's odyssey to the planet Jupiter concludes in an interface that makes man the paradigm of a race in some distant future, some distant place.

The future of man, *2001* suggests, is the future of interface. Anthropomorphism, man's innate self-absorption and tendency to ignore all but himself, is giving way (and by *2001* will have given way) to a perception of the processes that surround and create man. In *2001* men are not masters of the universe, as we would think today; they are simply creatures in the galactic ecology, drawn into a drama the scope of which they can scarcely recognize.

This book is an approach to interface, an attempt to view the processes generated by man's relationship to the contemporary technological environment. The theological consequences might not be so startling as those in *2001*, but then this book does not claim the foresight of the film. The chapters here will focus on common interfaces: cars, toys, television, machines. While the directions implicit in these chapters might become explicit in 2001, it is for us today to see and acknowledge them—we cannot afford the expense of waiting for tomorrow.

2

The Medium Is the Method

UNDERSTANDING INTERFACE

> It is quite possible that the next great age of science
> will be dedicated not to the study of the "outer" world of
> nature, nor to the "inner" world of the psyche, but to an
> exhaustive examination of those processes that take place at
> the interface between the biological/neural imprints and the
> stimuli that constantly bombard them.
>
> Don Fabun*

A developing consciousness of the presence and impact of technological change seems to be one of the hallmarks of our time. No sociological comment on the disruption of the family, the condition of the cities, or the failure of the schools fails to mention technological change as a major contributing factor. Indeed, the term "technological change" has the familiar ring of a mythical aphorism, an expression used frequently by just about everyone but understood largely in terms of its effects—and even then barely understood at all.

Theologians, representing the articulated consciousness of

* *The Dynamics of Change* (Englewood Cliffs, N.J.: Prentice-Hall, 1967), p. 12.

18

Christians, have recognized the eruptive forces of technological change but have done little to explore the significance of these forces for understanding the presence of Christians in today's world. In fact, technology has already made profound inroads on Christian experience: by surrounding man with images that reflect himself and not God, it has helped disseminate the sense of the sacred; by supplanting natural things with artificial things, it has made us aware that the traditional symbols no longer carry rich suggestive meanings. Indeed, technology has made Christians aware of the extent to which their environments shape religious consciousness.

However, the Christian theologian's reaction to technology itself has taken on little more articulation than an attempt, among the Catholics, to develop a better idea of man's creative role in shaping the world and, among the Protestants, to set forth a theology of hope. These limitations are understandable. Technology has not really raised theological questions as well as it has subtly avoided doing so. The frenetic efforts to propel giant rockets into space may well be deeply akin to the religious need to reach heaven; man may need to find norms by which he can judge his efforts to control the furious technological advances that seem runaway—but such questions are often hidden by the nature of technological change. The undecipherable ways in which technology affects men and the stubborn persistence of most thinkers (especially those committed to a religious credo) to follow older modes of thought have contributed to a distancing of theological activity from the mainstream of technological forces.

The failure can be understood on another level: technology itself is an enormously vast subject, highly difficult to conceptualize and treat intellectually. As Jacques Ellul, the most penetrating philosopher of technology, has written:

Since Technique has become the new *milieu,* all social phenomena are situated in it. It is incorrect to say that economics, politics, and the sphere of the cultural are influenced or modified *by* Technique; they are rather situated *in* it, a novel situation modifying all traditional social concepts. Politics, for example, is not modified by Technique as one factor among others which operate upon it; the political world is today defined *through* its relation to the technological society.*

Ellul gives quick and valuable perspective to the question of technology. To begin defining the problem in terms of "the impact of technology upon culture" is, as Ellul notes, futile: for technology (what he terms *Technique*) is already culture. Technology can be comprehended accurately only if it is equated with the contemporary environment.

All environments are special forms of communication: the world's letting man know who he is by his contact with it. Primitive man formed his sense of identity in terms of forces that he could not understand or affect; consequently his life was profoundly affected by the religious myths and rituals he constructed as a means of relating to these forces. Today feedback is a major process by which man discovers himself in relation to his environment. The question of the precise ways in which man is influenced by his environment has been neglected until recent efforts by anthropologists and ecologists—largely because man seems so adjustable to various environments that the impact of different geographical places or different environmental structures were not clearly noticeable. Yet the tchnological environment, by its pervasive nature, by its constant impingements on the awareness, and most especially by the effects it seemingly

* "The Technological Order." In Carl Stover, ed., *The Technological Order* (Detroit: Wayne State University Press, 1963), p. 11.

has had on such social experiences as the family, moral norms, and work, has made this consciousness of the effect of environment upon man a crucial problem for today.

In approaching the question of the technological environment, one must be wary. The tendency—as can be seen by the most familiar critics of technology (Ernst Juenger, for example, or Paul Goodman)—is to approach technology in terms of the ways it has deprived man of those values which are traditionally cherished: freedom, individual autonomy, spontaneity, personal development. Admittedly, an important characteristic of the technological environment is its highly manipulative nature: it tends to act upon man as a unit in a process. Consequently, to approach technology from the perspective of these values invariably means to condemn the environment out of which one speaks. Such condemnation may be correct, but it must be noted that the answer *has* been programmed into the question. To look for the direct moral effects of technology is to ask a wrongheaded question, for it amounts to contrasting the technological environment with the moral values which grew out of man's relationship to another environment—and like using numbers interchangeably with other symbols in mathematics, the terms do not match.

What *do* we know of the technological environment? How precise can we be in our formulation of the nature and processes of this environment? The best systematic treatment of the technological milieu is Jacques Ellul's *The Technological Society*. This book suggests by its own treatment the dangers and difficulties inherent in approaching the phenomenon of technology in America.

Ellul represents a long tradition of thought about technology which views the process of technological change as moving from the new technologies *to* society; though man is the shaper of his technologies, they are powerful in shaping him. This tradition contains two basic strains: the pessimistic strain, represented by theorists such as Ellul, Heidegger, and Ernst Juenger, and the optimistic strain, represented by men like B. F. Skinner. The "technology to man" tradition views man as a product of technology rather than technology as a product of man; their radical divergence comes in the ways they see technology affecting man—creating a utopian society or smothering the human spirit in a plastic universe.

One of the major themes that resounds through the writings of the "technologists" is the conviction that man is not very free to respond to a new environment. He is, in fact, as Skinner insists in *Walden II,* an organic function of the environment, and his behavior is capable of being programmed by the environment. Ellul's perspective is similar, if totally opposite in mood. Technique, which he describes as "the ensemble of practices by which one uses available resources in order to achieve certain valued ends," is identifiable with technology—and Technique is ultimately a destroyer of freedom. Technique defeats all but Technique. It becomes a common denominator: science, thought, political and religious efforts, focus everything upon method and tactics, rather than goals. Ellul's conception of Technique embraces everything from television advertising to programs in reading development; in all cases man becomes the victim, and not the beneficiary, of his own technology.

The other tradition concentrates on man rather than technology as the primal force. Again split into optimistic and pessimistic strains, this tradition assumes that man controls technology, rather than technology controlling man. C. Wright Mills represents the pessimistic strains of this tradition within American sociology; while his insights and conclusions parallel those of Ellul to a striking degree, his method differs radically. When

Mills, for example, analyzed the structures of power within a large organization, he identified many of the power struggles in terms almost synonymous with Ellul's "Technique"; nevertheless the focus remained on the people, not the techniques they employed, and the responsibilities for concentrated power were shown to belong to people, not techniques.

The optimistic strain in the man-to-technology tradition is represented by the numerous city planners and writers who are convinced that man can control the movement of technology. R. Buckminster Fuller, for example, while optimistic about the future of technology, views technological change as a spur to man's freedom rather than a hindrance.

The methodological difference between the technology-to-man tradition, which begins with a conception of technology and moves to man, and the man-to-technology tradition, which begins with the conditions of men's lives and moves to technological problems or possibilities, is a profound one. Invariably each tradition and each strain is going to reach conclusions modified by the values inherent in the premises. Ellul sees man as victimized by Techniques; Skinner sees the possibility of a technological utopia; Mills considers technology a complex of structures created by men largely for their own self-aggrandizement; Fuller considers technology to be beneficial for man, widening rather than constricting his freedom.

It seems that both approaches to technology—technology to man or man to technology—fail to comprehend their own limitations—that is, their inherent emphasis upon one polarity of the man-technology tension. A major problem of both traditions is their commitment to presumed values, a commitment so strong that the interpretations usually reflect these values more sharply than the descriptions in which, supposedly, these values are shown to emerge from the process. Consequently, Ellul's analysis of Technique, while brilliant, seems dominated by his distress with it; the same is true of Mills—and, from an optimistic point of view, of Skinner and Fuller.

Since the medium, as ever, is the method, the great question facing anyone concerned about technology today is primarily a methodological one; what method best enables us to understand the actual relationship between technology and man?

The opening chapter anticipated the method of interface. Interface is the process of interplay between man and environment; as such, an interpretation of interface is not inherently committed to value judgments—nor does it tend to be essentially man-centered or overly centered on technology. Consider a man riding a bicycle. He has a complex relationship to the two-wheeled vehicle on which he sits. While he "controls" the bike by moving the pedals and steering, he nonetheless must constantly respond to the feedback he senses in the very movement and tendencies of the bike. In technical jargon, he must learn to monitor feedback and adjust. He must be constantly aware of the information sent to him by the bicycle and respond accordingly.

This example offers some valuable insights into the process of interface. Note that once he is started, he does not have the freedom to suddenly "stop." Not that he is dominated by the bike; he is involved in the process which has been initiated by combining with it, and the process cannot immediately be halted. Eventually it can, though only through sensitive awareness of feedback and response. Moreover, his relationship to the bicycle both increases and decreases his freedom: it increases it by enabling a wider and faster scope of movement but decreases it by committing the rider to the bike.

The rider-and-bike example is admittedly a minute instance of the man-technology tension, but perhaps because it is so minute it suggests the limitations of the two major traditions to understand its meaning. Those who say technology operates on man would hardly be capable of convincing the rider that he is being controlled by his bike, and not vice versa. On the other hand, those who claim than man can control technology seem to think more in terms of the maker of the bike than the rider; the interpretations of this last class too often have a ring of decisive finality about them, without a sense of the precarious interplay of man and machine needed to keep technology, like the bicycle, steadily on course.

The following chapters will focus on man's relationship to technology as the bicycle rider feels it. Their method will be the interface between man and a particular technological environment—the demands and possibilities and the synergetic outcome of the combination, that is, an outcome different from any anticipated combination of man and the new environment. Rather than engage in hasty polemics for or against the environments, we will simply suggest ways of becoming more aware of the interface, and therefore helping the bike rider to steer. The suggestions, generally, are limited to some of the more striking theological implications of the technological environment.

The only significant thinker who has focused on the interface in recent years is Marshal McLuhan. McLuhan's analysis of the effects of print on three centuries is an admirable example of interface scholarship. McLuhan's method, it should be noted, is not nearly so firm and dogmatic as that of other thinkers on technology mentioned above. The "probe" enables McLuhan to touch on the right questions without being sure he has all the right answers. Actually it is the only method that fits the interface experience, which is too tentative and too dynamic to lend itself to an exhaustive treatment like Ellul's *The Technological Society*.

One of the most important advantages of emphasizing interface is that it keeps alive a consciousness of technology as participating in a reality larger than itself. Ellul's tendency to make Technique autonomous and unrelated to the spontaneous and nontechnical aspects of human experience shows the dangers of concentrating too strongly upon the technological environment alone. Interface can provide a much needed perspective for comprehending technology.

Among themselves, interfaces are synergetic. Historically, the electronics revolution spawned not only radio but talking movies, television, and computers. To analyze the way in which each of these media acts upon men independently of the others is to ignore the fact that their action is, in terms of people's lives today, simultaneous and multiple. What synergetic relationships exist are admittedly complex and difficult to ascertain; McLuhan, again, has attempted to describe some of these effects, and his work is, as he himself emphasizes, uncertain pioneering.

The interface experience is very much an experience of feedback. Every environment created by man acts as something of a shattered mirror, in which a man experiences multiple instances of feedback from himself, which he consequently interprets— consciously or unconsciously. This act of interpreting what the environment is relating to him constitutes an important aspect of the interface experience. Driving a car, for instance, a man is kept aware of his power to move this heavy object in any direction and at a variety of speeds. Such a reassurance of power is one of the most important forms of feedback from the automobile and a major characteristic of the automobile interface.

Not only does the interface provide man with feedback; he depends on this feedback and expects it from the technological environment. Ancient man was constantly reacting to the messages he received from the primitive environment by worshiping the gods who instigated the rain, the wind, the night. The technological environment has gradually distanced men from the direct experience of natural change, creating instead an environment which tells man far more about himself than about the gods. There is a kind of social self-knowledge possible—indeed, inescapable—in the technological world in which man is constantly bombarded with his own image and his own values.

There is no clear, easy way to approach interfaces. The actual interface may occur in a semiconscious way (as in a telephone conversation) or may intrude upon consciousness only dimly (as in driving a car). An important clue is to locate the mode of consciousness engendered by an interface—a daily, simply offhand way of thinking which apart from the interface would not exist. Another clue is to notice the slightly different ways in which man accustoms himself to an aspect of the technological environment, how over a few years the airplane or television takes on a qualitative difference in the lives of a large number of people.

Theologically, the interface is especially valuable because it focuses on a dimension of man's existence too little understood by theologians in the past: man's relationship with his total environment. The important historical religions, especially Christianity, have grown and matured on the basis of a consciousness of man in relation to God and in relation to his fellow man. The world has taken on value as the stage upon which the drama of religious life occurs. The important theological categories have emphasized man's relation to himself or to God: sin, guilt, faith, love, hope. The Pauline doctrine of redemption embraces all of creation; but neither in Paul nor in the tradition growing from Paul is man's precise relation to the scope of created reality explored in depth.

Of course, that the dimension of man's relationship to the whole of his environment would be neglected historically is understandable. An important characteristic of the technological environment is that it prods a consciousness of man's relationship to the world about him in a sharper, more intense way than ever before. Environmental consciousness exists today in a way that it has not since men had almost no role in shaping their environment and were constantly overwhelmed and awed by the world. The presence of this consciousness should be the forerunner of theological attempts to understand its meaning for man today.

To approach the question diagramatically, historical Christianity has thought of man within a triangular framework: the individual, the human community, and God. The consciousness of environment and its "massaging" effects upon man has, however, opened a new dimension to the framework. The triangular conception of life can no longer adequately express the total scope of Christian existence in today's world. A quadrilateral, or rectangular, conception is necessary, including the presence of the total—and today the technological—environment. This presence has always been admitted implicitly in the use of natural symbols within liturgy and in the recognition of God through cathedrals and works of art. But theology has only rarely explored the environmental interface in all its significance for Christian life.

The questions which emerge today from a rectangular conception of Christian existence are enormous in their range. It is not simply a matter of seeing, for example, nuclear weapons in a fresh light, but of recognizing the profound interrelationships between faith and the interface experience; between sacrament and interface; between human freedom and the innate tendency of technology to manipulate those associated with it.

By admitting the existential pervasiveness of environment, the Christian is in effect committing himself to a paradoxical conception of his relationship to the world: he admits his existence within it but insists on maintaining a critical distance to understand what it is doing to him, what effect the interfaces are having. The fundamental medieval conception of the Christian within time but not constricted by time takes on a fresh significance today: massaged by the environment, he nevertheless retains the freedom to step aloof from the environment, to comprehend its impact upon him. The impact is there: he cannot escape that. He can, however, respond to it, asserting autonomy in the throes of manipulation, faith in the presence of scientism and functionalism. He can above all draw from his faith and his community the strength and the insight to live a viable human life within a technological world—where human life is constantly threatened by the objectivizing tendencies of Technique.

What is at stake, finally, is the articulation of a badly needed Christian anthropology, which defines the whole man not in spite of the tendencies of the contemporary environment but largely in terms of them. The interface can make or destroy man. A sociologist like Mills and a philosopher like Ellul both seem convinced that today's interfaces are destroying, not creating, man. The task of the Christian may well be to discover how the interface can make, and not destroy, its human participant.

The purpose in the remaining chapters is to explore a few ways in which the interface experience can be understood from a Christian viewpoint, and in which might consist an effective Christian response. The work of developing a viable Christian anthropology for today and the near future is an extensive one. Nor is its main tool theology—the best efforts will happen among small groups, in experimental efforts to worship in terms of today's interfaces, in the attempts of Christians to react vitally to what is happening to them.

The approach taken in what follows, hopefully, will be true to the nature of the interface experience. Rather than developmental, these analyses will be exploratory, treating each interface separately and not attempting to foist a theological schema upon experience which exists in another context. Since the interface does raise a number of significant theological questions, the latter part of the book has been designed to emphasize the theological—rather than the anthropological—significance of interface.

The conclusions, like the method, will be exploratory and tentative. They are justified as much by making sense in terms of the interface experience as by their theological validity. Many conclusions will amount to little more than fresh questions, but then, this is the nature of the interface experience.

3

The Interface as Play

TOYS

With Charlie Brown, flying a kite is an emotional experience.

Violet,
in Charles Schulz's *Peanuts*

There was a stage, in the Barbie doll craze of several years ago, in which parents and psychologists began to join in protest against the Barbie invasion. Mattel's new doll universe had become an expensive one to populate and clothe—and the TV commercials made it seem imperative to little girls that they play God. The real meat of the protest wasn't as much in the expense of the dolls, however, as in their highly sophisticated designs. Barbie wasn't a mommy or baby doll; she was a swinging teen-age doll with a suitable entourage of boyfriends. She could dance, walk gracefully to an important social event, kiss; she was, as a psychologist writing for *Ramparts* put it, a way of experiencing the sex life of a teen-age girl despite being ten years younger.

Dangerous? Perhaps as much as some of the sophisticated toy weapons sold for boys the same age. Miniature ICBM's with launchers and cap warheads; a veritable arsenal from der-ringer to tommy gun—all available at the local dime store. Psy-chologists have long debated whether such toys aggravate or sublimate instinctive violent energies. As with the Barbie doll, nobody seems to know for sure.

Perhaps the confusion comes from asking the wrong ques-tion—or interpreting the child-toy interface in the wrong light. The success of the Barbie dolls seems to lie in their sophistica-tion: a wardrobe of contemporary fashions (mini-skirts and mini-mini-skirts for the more daring little girls), a universe built around Barbie (sound psychology there), even the hint of ten-sions with her parents. In playing Barbie, girls faithful to the instructions of the TV commercials were able to simulate an authentic environment—both social and psychological. Such play might not necessarily have had the effect of destroying the vitality of that environment when they reached it themselves—on the contrary, it may have been the training necessary to enable them to survive the future environment with grace.

Historically, toys have had two related functions in the growth of children: imitation and instruction. Toys have been a way of discovering in play the contours and the reciprocal patterns of the environment. By imitating his father's skill in building a hut, the child in a nomadic tribe builds a little hut for fun—yet his growing skill in learning to build is imperative for the future of the tribe. The kitten plays with a ball of yarn because it someday will become a mouse.

It would seem that the child-toy interface has not been trans-formed so radically by technology as other environmental inter-faces have been. In a sense this is true: children can accept a battery-operated robot far more calmly than their parents may one day accept the real thing. Yet the two essential features of today's child-toy interface—the meshing of technology with play and the fresh demands of a technological environment for an education commensurate with the contours of that environment—demand a serious look at the child-toy interface and its consequences.

New technological discoveries have always found an immediate market in toys. A clay animal on wheels was found in a Mexican culture which had no other evidence of wheels; the wheel was ready for a toy but not for the larger social tasks too dependent on entrenched patterns to permit a revolution like the wheel. The first fifty years of the motion picture are the history of a toy—early forms like the thaumatrope discs or the zoetrope were fancy toys that gave the illusion of movement. Toys have never demanded great sophistication in design—and this is far more important—the revolution in social and economic patterns which larger technological innovations create.

In this sense, new technologies have always been welcomed as a form of play, whereas they have not always been welcomed as a new form of work. As a plaything a new technology has two advantages: that of the novelty, something prized highly by children, but likewise that of creating for them new levels of involvement, new sources of power and control.

Suppose a child receives for a gift a remote-controlled robot that will roll in whatever direction the child chooses, scoop objects into his shovel hands, replace them elsewhere, and blink the bulb above his head if he gets stuck. Lots of fun—even the least imaginative child would have no difficulty in finding things for his robot to do. The thrill of such a robot lies as much in its novelty as in the capacities for power it gives the person holding the control box. The point of such an interface is that the child is discovering something his parents might balk at were the robot four feet taller and more sophisticated: the excitement and fun in discovering a new range of power.

Play acts as the least disturbing introduction to a new kind of interface. The ratios of power, prejudices about human involvement, and sensibilities are not firmly set in a child; he is open to anything—and as technology advances, "anything" is the only limit to be placed on the possible toys.

A child, for example, is given a bicycle. He has seen the older children wheeling around the neighborhood but has never quite identified with them enough to attempt getting on top of one himself. Now his parents are waiting, and he feels courageous enough to try. Suddenly he is sitting atop the bicycle and finding the pedals with his feet. The world looks different beneath him. He can move as he never could before. In minutes he learns the intricate feedback system the wobbling motion of the bike gives him. What might represent on another level a threat for his father (who might need to learn the operation of a new machine or fly a large plane) becomes for the child with a bike simple fun.

In a tribal age the future of a society depended on children's playing with bows and arrows, a canoe, a thatched roof of a make-believe hut. Recent Western civilization, with its insistence on specialization and economically feasible skills, has degenerated the vital role of play and siphoned the supposedly important features of education into the classroom. Today, with a technological world the greatest threat to man's sanity and his future, the pendulum has gone full swing. It may be far more important that Johnny learns to play with a battery-operated robot than that he learn his ABC's. By the time he is out of school a specialized skill will not help him live as a human being so much as will an awareness of the proportions and demands of his environment. And the schools, constructed around a language-oriented idea of education, are incredibly distant from introducing him to the scale and dimensions of the environment he will one day inhabit.

This is the first important consequence of the contemporary toy interface: complex technological toys are as indispensable for today's children as a bow and arrow are for a child in a hunting tribe.

The second consequence seems almost the same as the first: the nature of play needs to be reflected in technological toys. One of the grave challenges which today's children will face is that of increased leisure; technology, especially automation, will free people for more play. Adults, as well as children, are being forced to discover the possibilities for play in technology. To some extent they already have: ads and commercials depict the automobile as a plaything more than as a serious mode of transportation. Speedboats, little twin-engine airplanes, and motorcycles are selling as never before. But the opportunities for play provided by technology delineate a far wider ambit than these. It seems that relatively few technological forms of recreation offer the chance of that creative interplay between man and machine which can serve as the best education to a technological environment.

For play, as Johan Huizinga, author of *Homo Ludens,* has observed, is a profoundly serious thing. But not in the experience—though poker or college football can become deadly serious forms of play—so much as in the impact it makes on man. Just as sports give the body tone, shape, and muscle, interface play can give the psyche a healthy sense of the interface and its possibilities. Not only does the man with the motorboat sense his own power; he likewise comes to respect the power of the engine and the ways in which it can move the boat. That delicate interplay between man and machine—amounting almost to a conversation—constitutes an indispensable sensibility for man living in a technological world. Without such a sensibility, he will feel uneasy with technology, either its psychological victim or its furious master. And such a sensibility is far more easily developed in play than in work.

A third observation about the play interface applies especially to children. Play forms have not only educated them to the demands and contours of an environment but have been subtle training in motivation as well. Sports, for example, are probably a major training ground for the competitive instincts that need to be unleashed in a capitalistic society. Sports are likewise excellent preparation for teamwork, a feature which has become more important for the contemporary businessman than the lust for competition. Toys also affect and train motivations: the toy gun is just as much a means of self-assertion for a seven-year-old as it is for the television hero, whose identity sits ominously in his holster. Model trains, so popular a decade ago, have yielded to tracks with remote-controlled cars which can be raced—with impressive similarities to the actual conditions of auto racing. A child has a chance to learn early that the car is a plaything, a dangerous but exciting toy.

In all three effects of the toy interface, a vital trend can be seen for the future, a trend with significant repercussions for the Christian community. As the technological environment becomes more inescapable, more tightly woven into the fabric of all human activities, it is vital that men be able to live humanly—through, and not despite, the burgeoning interfaces. The twin problem of increasing technology and increasing leisure meets in the interface as play: technology as a way for man to find himself and the dimensions of his interfaces with the new environment.

The identity of the Christian, as much as the identity of any totally human citizen of a technological society, will depend increasingly upon this ability to live with the new technologies in style and with grace. The play interface illuminates aspects of the new environment and introduces men to fresh ways of relating to these environments without great discomfort; the play interface, in almost all cases, humanizes.

Three consequences of the play interface for Christians of the future can be identified. The first, and surely the most imperative, is the need for persons to create themselves through play rather than work. The legacy of Christianity, most especially post-Reformation Christianity, has bound men ethically to a spiritual growth dependent on work. Even the earliest monastic credo, St. Benedict's *ora et laboris*, stressed work over leisure—though attempting to create a synthesis of the two. The heirs to the Reformation solidly implanted in the Protestant sects a profound conviction that work—more than prayer, more even than social conscience—assures salvation. Work became the measure and goal of human life and human striving; more to the point, it became the criterion for personal growth.

A technological environment not only supplants forms of human energy; it tends to supplant the motivations for these energies. "Work" is still considered essential—if not absolutely necessary for a meaningful life. But the era of totally automated processes of providing for most basic needs is, if not distinctly in sight, acknowledged by many planners as being imminent. Even today the widespread phenomenon of moonlighting suggests that people are more dependent upon activity they identify as work than upon the paycheck an extra job brings in. People want to work because they feel they need to work. In actuality that very need, more strongly felt today than in centuries past, may be a potent reaction to the usurpation—and threat of greater usurpation—of work by technology.

There is no way of knowing what psychic destruction follows as a result of the frenetic desire to work in a world in which the demand for work is, like the work itself, being sapped of its human vitality and appeal. The distance between a man crafting his own weapons and furniture is worlds apart from a man twisting a cylinder on an assembly line. The distance becomes even greater as the man has only to keep track of dials and lights on instruments. A man becomes no longer a worker in the primitive sense but a guardian of a process. The time put in and the paycheck may still be there but not the satisfaction of doing something, of changing something with his own hands or mind. The need to work is degenerated into the need to do something for which there is some payment. And the stronger the need, the greater the potential frustration.

Moving from an ethics of work to an ethics of leisure can—and no doubt will—be achieved far more easily by a fresh generation than by fresh outlooks on the part of teachers, pastors, and others responsible for shaping attitudes. What is imperative is that the new attitude be more than a renunciation of the work ethic, that it be a clear and meaningful pursuit of personal fullness through the possibilities inherent in leisure—and not the substitution of some bland idolatry of nonactivity.

Here the interface with technological toys is especially instructive. As play, interface activity can be one of the best ways by which man can accommodate himself comfortably to a technological environment. Technological toys may be the most important preparation for a world in which leisure needs as much, if not more, status than work; but they are definitely one form of such preparation, and an important one.

A related consequence of the toy interface is the way in which it makes new experiences and new methods acceptable. The term "novelty" has a tinge of negative connotation to anyone but a child, who is wise enough to relish new experiences, fresh changes in the world about him. As technological change brings in its wake increasing upheavals, men are going to have to learn to live with things that they do not understand, things that give them a breadth of power they have never known before. Toys whose appeal is largely in their novelty may well be the harbingers of the great experiments of the next decade; and the children who respond to those (or similar) innovations as toys may well be best capable of responding to them as serious alternations in the environment.

The capacity to survive as men in a world in which technological interfaces occupy energies and consciousness at every turn depends on the ability to comprehend and even enjoy these interfaces. If the interface exists only out of felt necessity—whether economic or whatever—the whole man will not, cannot, be involved. For men to be creative within a technological environment, they must learn the ways of creating themselves through the interfaces—through the forms of play which the interfaces make possible. Toys have been and will remain children's playthings; hopefully, though, in an age of spiraling technologies, we can all learn again how to play as children.

4

The Toy We Never Play With

THERMONUCLEAR WEAPONRY

> The Bomb's the thing
> Wherein we'll catch the conscience of the king.
> Freely adapted from Shakespeare,
> Hamlet, Act II, Scene ii

In the last chapter it was suggested that the toy is one of the best introductions to our interface situation with a technological world. Toys are a special kind of education via interface; they give us a chance to become acquainted with an environment and the demands and possibilities of that environment before its dangers and responsibilities become real. Eskimo children learn to spear fish with toy spears: for them it is a game, a toy; for the tribe it is a matter of life or death.

For most of us, the Bomb has been the great toy by which we have learned to live with technology as a force of unlimited proportions. Experience of the Bomb has ushered in a consciousness of our technological situation perhaps impossible any other way. For technology is fundamentally designed and controlled power, power to change physical objects, power to manipulate other technological forms—and, soon enough, power to manipulate man. We have long known technology as a convenience, and secondarily as a threat. But our survival on this planet, it is becoming increasingly apparent, is going to lie in our learning to live with the enormous possibilities of power which technology has spawned. The Bomb has taught us something of this, and it continues to teach us.

To be sure, the Bomb is the one toy we need to keep in the closet. We played with it once, when it had just been introduced to us and its allure was irresistible—just as a ten-year-old, given a motorcycle through some crude mistake, might try that: once. Ever since, we have kept it hidden from sight, with the very knowledge of its presence behind closed doors our real interface with it. No child, we knew, could play with that toy without destroying himself and others with him. But we had to be told about the Bomb, and wise fingers kept pointing to it reminding us that it was there. Really, it is our only forbidden toy, but the one that we seem most conscious and anxious about. In a way, we are aggravated that it was ever made, yet—in that it has introduced us to the era of nuclear technology—somehow thankful of its presence.

Certainly the Bomb *is* no toy, even though its use in international affairs has had the appearance of a prop in some gigantic game. Substantially our interface with the Bomb has operated the same way that a dreaded toy can work upon a child, for nuclear weapons have educated us to the real proportions of our environment—proportions that the schools scarcely recognize and are incapable of comprehending. Of all the various interfaces with our technological world, the one between man and Bomb has been the most spectacular, and has engendered the most fear.

For all of us, nevertheless, the Bomb is the most distant technological environment. We drive cars and cannot cross a street without retaining a consciousness of their power; we use telephones, radio, and television as normally as we would a can opener. But the Bomb lies hidden in the closet; it takes an incident like the crash of a loaded B-52 to remind us that it is there. Its potential effects, as depicted in a shocking film like *The War Game,* startle and terrify us. We fear it, but the fear itself is elusive and nameless: not only are a few lives (including, perhaps, our own) threatened, but the future of spaceship earth. That thousands of millions of years of evolution could lead to such an absurd cataclysm is the final fear; for here a single life is not threatened, or even the life of a nation, but a much more precious hope, the meaning of life itself.

The first and most immediately obvious effect of the Bomb is the psychological atmosphere it has created: a spirit of suppressed terror. The fear hangs over all discussion of war and Vietnam like a pall; it has helped instill in the youth of the sixties a gripping realism and a vague premonition of hopelessness. The fear has likewise stoked a latent sensibility that thrives on violence; almost as an instinctive, defensive reaction, violence becomes more acceptable—a common theme to films, drama, and television shows, not as much for the purpose of revealing the human wellsprings of violence as for satisfying the taste for violence fostered, not to say created, by the Bomb.

But a more significant aspect of the interface with the Bomb is the disposition toward technology which it engenders. It is here that the Bomb has "educated" us to technology—but in such a way as to make us more fearful of it than confident in it, more convinced of its uncanny power than its enormous benefits.

Much of the discussion on the year 2000 has emphasized our attitude of wonderment and gratitude toward technology, envisioning a world of instant personal communication via telephone-television, a world without traffic jams because business centers have been disintegrated by the new communications networks. But there has been another, less noticeable, strain in the discussion, one which senses the dangers of our accelerating technologies. *The President's Analyst,* a cleverly satirical film, concludes with the discovery of a power that intends to take over the world, a power that has a better chance than Russia and China combined: The Telephone Company, only plugged-in automatons receiving their instructions from another plugged-in automaton. The familiar literary theme of the monster destroying its creater—from Prometheus to Frankenstein to Capek's *R.U.R.*—has become a vital motif in our attitude toward technology. Thanks to the Bomb.

The forbidden toy, then, has forced us to think deeply about technology, if only in the direction of its destructive capacities. In his book *On Aggression* Konrad Lorenz shows that men and rats are the only animals that destroy their own kind with any frequency or with a lack of significant provocation. The Bomb, even more than the reminder of wars, forces us to focus on man's innate capacity for murder. Like all technological environments, the Bomb reflects aspects of man that he would usually prefer to keep will hidden. What the Bomb says about the nation which first created it, and the men who believe in it, is roughly as disturbing as what an afternoon of television game shows and soap operas say about the people who create and watch them.

·Perhaps finally the most important lesson of our interface with the Bomb is the recognition that we have passed the time when technologies had interchangeable uses and weapons could be muted to serve humane purposes. Primitive weapons were primarily extensions of agricultural and hunting tools. In Assam the knife was used to fell trees, animals, and enemies. The gradual sophistication of weapons throughout history has made them increasingly specific in the kind of work they will do. Discarded army tanks don't even do a good job of pressing down newly seeded ground. As weapons became increasingly specific and potent in their purposes, their advantages for other areas of technology waned. So man learns through weapons a critical truth about technology: that sophistication destroys the possibility of interchangeability—that subsequently there cannot even be the temptation to turn swords into plowshares. An ICBM warhead might conceivably displace an inconvenient mountain, but only at the cost of poisoning the air within hundreds of miles. The only use for weapons is the use they were built to serve: destruction—of enemy soldiers, artillery, villages, women, children, civilization. Modern weapons, especially the Bomb, pose to men a chilling parable; and the meaning of that parable is that power can no longer be judged by a generalized effect (in, say, horsepower) so well as by specialized purpose. How many men will it kill? How far will the winds carry its death?

Psychologically, this truth about modern technology may contradict the rational response by depending, for security, upon stockpiling and fantastic allocations in weapons research. It is not so much that people want to use technology to destroy others, simply that the discomfort the Bomb has created prompts an almost psychotic desire for more and better bombs, weaponry so sophisticated that its use guarantees wholesale death— and its existence almost guarantees that someday it will be used. Only a few centuries ago, weapons could be turned aside and used for peace; swords could be melted, guns could be used strictly for hunting. We face today a drastically new interface and, as a result, the unceasing peril of devastating war.

The great responsibility men have in facing the dreaded closet door is to learn elsewhere what they already have learned from the Bomb—the proportions of technological power. The attitude toward technology engendered by the Bomb is essentially negative and fearful, almost nihilistic; we have come to revere technology more for its destructive than its creative possibilities. Surely much has been made of the creative potential in technology, but quite often in terms that show a disregard for the real meaning of human life as banal as the Bomb's respect for life.

Buckminster Fuller, perhaps the most articulate and profound exponent of the positive possibilities of technology, has suggested an understanding of future technology which provides a positive alternative to the fear inspired by the Bomb. Fuller conceives of evoluting (in preference to "evolving") technology as a means of getting more and more from less and less. The population may expand in geometric ratios, but so, insists Fuller, does technology. Technological power may be awesome, yet that awesomeness should be an incentive to manage and direct it, not to fear and back away from it. Significantly, Fuller, born in the nineteenth century, developed many of his ideas before the era of nuclear weaponry. Yet his understanding of technology and its possibilities for dealing with the most critical problems of future decades—food, shelter, and substantial education for everyone—lack the gilded optimism of today's technological utopians.

The nuclear bomb astounds us by making technological use of primal energy dynamics. "If man is to demonstrate any important mastery of his universe," Fuller suggests, "then all the fundamental behavior phenomena of his dynamic universe—as demonstrated in the 92 (atomic) primary team plays—must be involved directly or indirectly in the process." Three steps are involved in a technological mastery of the universe: first, com-

prehending the synergetic principles governing the universe—
that is, understanding the parts through their relationship to the
whole. Second, man must find the most economical ways possible of transforming these system relationships to work. Third,
he must master the principles that govern the evolution of patterns and the more subtle, offbeat relationships which these
patterns affect—patterns as simple, for example, as the systematic displacement of water when a stone is thrown into a pond.

One of the crucial and encouraging aspects of Buckminster
Fuller's vision is its capacity to respect the possibilities of technological power, but with the difference that the respect hasn't
come from the Bomb. Fuller's work is not overcast with that
aura of fear, the almost worshipful respect, which the Bomb
has brought for most of us. He terms his efforts, revealingly,
"comprehensive, anticipatory design science"—a science which
deals with total integrities, major synergetic patterns. Fuller's
confidence in the innate friendliness of the universe almost
smacks of a Teilhardian faith, the major difference perhaps being that Fuller's vision keeps a solid scientific grounding at
every moment.

Fuller's thought gives us a far-reaching vision of technology
while short-cutting the interface with nuclear weaponry. Just to
think about technology with a viewpoint that doesn't keep our
eyes fixed on the dreaded closet door is an enormous advantage,
for it enables us to cast off the fears that the Bomb has created.
Technological power should not terrify men into spiritual paral-
ysis, nor should it intimidate the efforts of those who are not
terrified. Nevertheless, responsibility and caution should characterize efforts to take advantage of the patterns and energy structures in the universe, and Fuller, perhaps more than anyone
else today, offers a viable course along which this can happen.

5

From Buick to Volkswagen

THE GLORY AND THE POWER

> There are two things no man will admit he can't do well:
> drive and make love.
>
> Stirling Moss*

"Men who follow the herd," we are informed by a recent ad, "would probably feel out of character in a Toronado. . . . Toronado isn't likely to appeal to every Tom, Dick or Harry. Which is really one of its biggest appeals."

Of such stuff are car ads in America made—and through such stuff are million of cars and the beliefs invested in those cars sold annually. What was once called the horseless carriage, a radically new form of transportation, has become a major insignia of technological society—and one of the most potent sources of change in man's condition.

A brief survey of car ads is reason enough to question the real nature of the car-man interface today:

Chrysler Imperial: "As the miles flick by, relax. Assume a new position. Re-adjust the optional six-way power seat so that seat height, tilt, and leg room are right for you."

---

* In *Man And Motor: The Twentieth Century Love Affair,* edited by Derek Jewell (New York: Walker & Co., 1967).

Cadillac Eldorado: "Only one car can make a Cadillac owner look twice."

Pontiac: "When you're ready to give up ordinary driving and graduate to Wide-Tracking, turn to a GTO."

Plymouth Fury III: "Luxury isn't expensive anymore."

Porsche: "A Porsche is so responsive to your touch, it seems to read your mind. You can almost *think* it through a turn. It drives the way you feel like driving: calmly competent on the way to work, razor-sharp and aggressive on racing weekends. Whatever your mood, this car instinctively matches it."

Chrysler: "Newport to New Yorker. The '68 Chryslers are here. Make your move. Then sit back, and watch your friends watch."

Advertising, thanks to the volume of money and resources spent yearly on research, is a vital index to the interfaces between man and the commodities advertising promotes. But the contents of an ad or a commercial for a car are not nearly so revealing as the assumptions underlying those contents. Chrysler Imperial believes that absolute comfort is possible—and more significantly, desirable—anywhere. Cadillac assumes that cars are built to look at—certainly a valid assumption, but likewise an indulging one. Pontiac implies that "ordinary driving" is something of an apprenticeship to real, or "Wide-Track," driving. The Porsche copy, describing a Porsche as a mechanical alter ego, strikes perhaps the most deeply. Why, after all, *do* people buy cars? Why do they drive them miles farther than necessary when simple convenience or economics would suggest walking or public transportation?

The interface between car and man is one of the more characteristic and complex psychological events of the twentieth century. Its inherent complexity is created by the nearness and personal character of the interface: a car, unlike a plane or a building, belongs to a person, at most a family. Its closed space, its mobility, and its spatial autonomy give it individual character. Its relationship to man does not lend itself to easy generalization, because each man establishes his own relationship with his own car. Indeed, that very relationship and the possibilities of that relationship are a most vital source today for believing in and asserting personal autonomy.

The car-man interface can be understood from two directions: in terms of the levels of relationships (the car as image of the person, as companion, as sensual gratification, etc.) and likewise in terms of the effects upon man (the experience of power, the sense of freedom, engendered by a car). Neither direction, interestingly, has received much attention by anyone other than those who make and sell the cars.

The levels of relationships are revealed with some thoroughness by the ads and commercials. The most frequently suggested mode of relationship—the car as an image of the person—is handled in a thousand subtle ways. "Status" once had clearly defined terms and limits. The car, more than any other symbol of status, has confused the meaning of status by making it available to anyone. Cadillacs can be found on the streets of an inner-city ghetto. The car serves as an outer skin, a way of stating to the world the image that a person wants the world to identify with him. A striking Ford Mustang commercial made in 1965 depicted "Harry," quiet antique shop proprietor, on his lunch hour. Outside of the shop Harry doffed a sports hat, took off his coat to reveal a blazing red vest, and hopped into a bright red Mustang. Harry was transformed, presumably by the Mustang. Over the hills he went, to a quiet, shady spot in a field where a spread lunch awaited him—next, of course, to a beautiful young woman with open arms. Change your image—perhaps your identity—Ford suggests: drive a Mustang.

Recent advertising for cars has depended largely on photography (some of it the most remarkable being used in ads or commercials) to suggest the physical beauty of a car, and it has depended on ad copy or commercial commentary to describe "performance." A car may be externally sleek or streamlined or vigorous, but the way it hugs curbs, barrels into 90 miles an hour within seconds, and quiets all sounds other than the four-speaker stereo tape outfit matters too: this is essential to the image, that the image accurately reflects the real (or believed to be real) him.

It remains to the psychologists, perhaps of a generation after which the car has become unnecessary, to probe the importance of the car for modern man in his search for (and frustration of) self-identity. The dependence on a mechanical instrument for self-identity reveals a dependence on technology which many would fear and many others would deny. Yet it can be wondered what small percentage of car owners look to their cars primarily as instruments for transportation; and it can be further questioned how much these people are in touch with the times. The automobile has become a central landmark in the contemporary psychological terrain.

If the car gives a man an opportunity to exhibit his self-image to others, it likewise serves to reinforce his own sense of personal power. This second relationship to his car becomes more complex than that of the self-image. The power of the individual is one of those quiet, unmuttered assumptions which has grown with the history of political democracies. The term "freedom" as used in the American Constitution contains significant assertions of power. Political freedom in a democracy means, concurrently with liberty, some grip on the sources of power. Decision-making belongs to the populace, not to the few. The small community in American history, the town meeting, the growth of journalism and the print media, helped insure this sense of personal participation in political and social power. Horatio Alger symbolizes success, but included in that success is the growth of personal power.

The twentieth century, however, has been dominated increasingly by technological growth. And it is a key postulate of technological development that it tends to diffuse and relocate power. Bosses give way to managers. Decision-making becomes a method of identifying the proper response within a totally programmed process. Most critical of all, people in every aspect of their lives lose the vital contact with the decisions and changes affecting their lives. Vietnam and poverty, as pressing as they are considered by the media, engender apathy, largely because the possibilities of asserting personal or social power no longer exist as they once did.

The psychologists may suggest to what degree the automobile has mollified this reduction in a sense of power. Clearly, when cars built to move at 130 miles an hour sell better in large cities than small cars built to move at half that speed one's eyebrows are raised. The experience of power in a car may not be nearly as important for the owner of a GTO as the knowledge of the power his car contains. To know that the power is there—not necessarily to experience it, except perhaps at rare moments—is enough of a safeguard, enough of an assurance that the person still has some kind of power he can wield.

A third level of relationship can be seen in the car as companion, in some cases as alter ego. As an image of the self, the car reveals its owner's chosen identity to others; as a source of power, it soothes his own incapacity for power. As a companion, it serves to participate in a relationship which the driver can control entirely, a relationship which can be automatically satisfactory, built entirely around his own presumptions and demands.

In 1965 Chevrolet produced an award-winning commercial, entitled "Lazy Afternoon," for its luxury coupe Caprice. For three minutes a woman drives through a quiet summer landscape in a convertible. The images are lush and moody; the song implies a vivid, erotic relationship.

In terms of both companionship and sexual connotations, this commercial is rich in suggesting why a lady would *really* want the Caprice. As a companion, the car takes her wherever a whim determines. As an assurance of sexual identity, the car is stable, attractive, and obedient. It is a companionship and a sexual bond the terms of which she can dictate. Toronado ads insist that their cars are "broad-shouldered, massively male." The companionship proffered here is different; its appeal is to the man rather than to the woman, for the major sexual attraction of a car is in extending and confirming—not so much complementing—sexual identity.

The fourth level of relationship, the car as a kind of sexual assurance, exists in various subtle ways. Admittedly sex is used, in one way or another, to sell just about everything today—but with the car the sex-conscious adman has decided advantages. What sells a car, or any commodity, finally is not what the ad copy says or what the commercial depicts so much as the interface itself as someone experiences it, and the man-car interface is very sexual. Ernest Dichter, the depth psychologist who pioneered much of the motivational research for advertising agencies, used to say that a sporty convertible appeals to a man as a technological version of a seductive, easily accessible blonde.

But the average man would be less prone to buy the sports car, just as he would be less prone to marry the blonde.

The sexual aspect of the man-car interface does not work so simply, however. When a man gets into a car, he relates to it less with a distinct sexual attitude (as he would relate to a woman) than with a complex of sexual desires and inhibitions —mostly unconscious. The car tends to take on not a distinct, separate sexuality but a configuration capable of responding to the individual's sexual needs. Consequently interfaces differ enormously; a woman driving a station wagon experiences something much different (or at least much less) than a man in his Barracuda. Conversely, a woman might fight the closed space of a car, its mobility and its usually undemanding possibilities of power and speed, highly sexual.

All these four levels of relationship have one element in common: play. Even though highway deaths surpass 100,000 yearly, Americans ultimately do not take their cars seriously. A careful study of automobile commercials is proof enough that the car interface is actually quite similar to the toy interface. In car commercials the people are shown driving through empty highways on lovely days. They always seem to be at leisure—destination never matters nearly so much as the enjoyment of driving. The main appeal of the car itself lies in its presence: its shiny surface, its impressive color, its fascinating gadgets. Again the ad copy: "Luxury isn't expensive anymore." . . . "Whatever your mood, this car instinctively matches it." The car is America's favorite toy, its most dependable, fun, and available plaything. A toy, incidentally, which all ages seem to find equally fascinating.

These comments on the various levels of interface between man and the automobile could hardly cover the full gamut of the car interface. Indeed, one of the most important features of the man-car interface—the gestalt created of man and car—has hardly been treated here at all. The coming chapter on the man-machine gestalt will treat this question, an imperative one, for it, more than any of the features discussed here, embraces man and car into a third, synergetic whole.

6

The Motorcycle as Persona

THE MAN-MACHINE GESTALT

> It is not with metal that the pilot is in contact. Contrary
> to the vulgar illusion, it is thanks to the metal, and by virtue
> of it, that the pilot rediscovers nature.
>
> Antoine de Saint-Exupéry*

In classical Greek mythology one of the most illuminating symbols was the Centaur, a creature with the legs and torso of a
beast combined with the chest and head of a man. The Centaurs
were known as wild, incorrigible beings, man as confined to his
animal instincts and passions. The defeat of the Centaurs by the
Lapithae came to signify the conquest of civilization over primitive barbarism.

It is unfortunate that the mythology of our day—less visual
and less coherent than that of the Greeks—has not construed
for us an image of man analogous to the Centaur. If it did, the
result might be more grotesque than the Centaur, but just as
significant: a combination of man and machine, a combination
which dominates his world and increasingly his consciousness.

The man-machine interface is central to environmental ex-

* *Wind, Sand and Stars* (New York: Reynal and Hitchcock, 1939), p. 67.

perience in a technological world. Machines—extensions of man's limbs, energies, and senses—have widened the ambit of almost all human activity. Transportation depends not just on wheels but on a gas-fueled engine to move those wheels. Visual experience is increasingly dominated by a movie projector or a television tube. Movement in our large buildings depends on escalators and elevators.

It is probably true that we are entering an epoch in which the present man-machine ratio will be violently jolted by the computer—which is more of an automated brain than a machine. The computer will intervene between man and machine, widening the space of the interface. But in this sense the computer has not yet totally "arrived"—we still make the adjustments ourselves, turn the knobs, and sense at close range the power we can wield with a button, whether it be on a lawn mower or an assembly line production unit.

The man-machine interface is important for man today on several grounds: its inroads on him psychologically; its effects on his image of himself; the sense of power it has given him. Above all, however, the man-machine interface has confronted man with an image of himself loaded with repercussions: man as part of a larger gestalt—the man-machine gestalt.

Twentieth-century art has attempted to explicate this gestalt; both the cubist and the surrealist movements explored a psychological world of machines and the consequences of their geometric forms or inhuman rhythmic and corrupting possibilities for man. The Bauhaus, a German school for architects and designers at the beginning of the century, attempted to pioneer an industrial aesthetic: design accentuated function, not irrelevant features thought to be simply "beautiful." Plays, movies, and TV series have concentrated on the man-machine interface: from Karel Capek's robot-threatening *R.U.R.* (1920) to a TV series built around the man-machine relationship, *Mission: Impossible.* The gradual tendency has been to move from a sense of the machine as a threat to man's humanity and freedom to an awareness of it as a part of the human gestalt—as an indispensable aspect of contemporary human experience.

The man-machine gestalt can be identified with the man-machine interface. The gestalt can be highly synergetic: the combination of rider and motorcycle, for example, or pilot and aircraft creates the sense of a fresh, liberated identity. Antoine de Saint-Exupéry, the French poet-pilot, expressed something of this as few pilots have been able to, before or after him:

> The element smacks the sides of the hull with a sound like a gong, and the pilot can sense the tumult in the quivering of his body. He feels the ship charging itself with power as from second to second it picks up speed. He feels the development, in these fifteen tons of matter, of a maturity that is about to make flight possible. He closes his hand over the controls, and little by little in his bare palms he receives the gift of this power. The metal organs of the controls, progressively as this gift is made him, become the messengers of the power in his hands. And when his power is ripe, then, in a gesture gentler than the culling of a flower, the pilot severs the ship from the water and establishes it in the air.*

Yet even as the machine can expand and thrill man, it can diminish and psychologically castrate him. The history of the factories in the early decades of the industrial revolution leaves a ˉshuddering image of the man-machine interface. As long as machines were considered the important processes of production —and the men who ran the machines slaves to those processes

---

* *Ibid.*, pp. 72–73.

—men were economically and physically subordinated to their own inventions.

Like all other major interfaces, the man-machine gestalt has tended historically to have radically ambivalent effects: the machine has freed man of thoughtless labor, and it has made possible a richer world, but in the process it has stripped him of earlier assurances about himself and destroyed millions of men who lived in a system in which the machine—and not man—became the measure of what it would do.

The repercussions of the man-machine gestalt can be seen in three major areas: the impact of the machine upon the psyche of contemporary man, its effects on man's image of himself, and its modification of his sense of power. In each of these areas the man-machine interface has made significant inroads on man's sense of his present identity.

The psychological impact of the man-machine gestalt may well be the strongest of the three. Up to the industrial revolution man lived his long history in an environment fashioned more by nature than by himself. Suddenly, within the breadth of a century, the environment become drastically transformed. Urban centers changed from communities to sprawling, factory-dominated lands. Throughout the twentieth century, encounters and involvements with machines have become more commonplace to most people than encounters with natural objects. Water comes out of a faucet and is channeled usually into some mechanized device like a dishwasher. Most of an urban dweller's decisions about modifying his environment can be made by the flick of an electrical switch. The "world" is to the contemporary consciousness not a world of weather, trees, the elements, but a world of mechanized devices that may not be understood yet that serve consistently and efficiently.

Psychologically, what has this done to man? Theories abound, from the well-worked phrase of alienation to acknowledgments, in depth psychology, of machines offering man new possibilities for expressing sexual needs or the drive for power. Few psychologists, it seems, have considered the machine as a counterpart to man—a creature with whom he relates, creating the man-machine gestalt described earlier, as well as the tensions arising from this gestalt.

As a counterpart to man in a larger gestalt, the machine acts simultaneously as threat and friend. It does things which he cannot do or—in the case of the automatic dishwasher—which he would prefer not to do. As a purely servile, undemanding worker, it is clearly a convenience; and yet it would be simplistic to assume that its effects on man's psyche would stop here. A large, mechanized production unit in a factory, and even the dishwasher, holds a vague, if rarely conscious, threat to contemporary man: it is a symbol of his power over nature, but a power with which he feels uneasy—a power, certainly, which he does not understand. And who is to know where the machine will lead? Millions of American workers have already felt the nameless personal blight that automation brings in its wake—a threat which cannot be understood simply in economic terms but which had deep roots in the man-machine interface. The machine is a way of harnessing and directing energies, energies which have for centuries been a way of man's proving himself as a man.

Psychologically, the machine has taken on the identity of an intruder in the human community. And being a discontented, aggressive intruder, it has tried to reformulate some of the basic patterns of that community—to mixed reactions of gratitude and hostility. Men, even the technicians and designers of the machines, stand by with a feeling of uninvolvement in the processes the machines initiate and continue. And the intruder persists in his tumultuous work—barely understood, fought only with nervous reticence.

It is the very ambivalence of man's reactions to the machine —his gratitude and hostility, his enjoyment of the luxury it has brought him mixed with the fear of its dangers for his identity —which is the most striking psychological effect of the machine gestalt upon man. Derek Jewell noted, in his book perceptively titled *Man and Motor: The Twentieth Century Love Affair,* that the relationship between man and his car is actually a love-hate relationship—with all of the Freudian overtones. This is true of any relationship of contemporary man with a machine capable of noticeable power: the intruder is loved and hated at the same time.

The second effect of the man-machine gestalt is seen in a conflict of popular images of man—images formed by the media, man's perceptions, and his experiences. The images tend to exacerbate the effect of this ambivalence because they are often so bewildering. A number of images have emerged from the man-machine gestalt: man as conqueror of the earth, though gaining a fresh contact with it through the machine; man as a slave of the machine; man as a collaborator with the machine, not in creation but in destruction.

Each of these images has vital sources in popular literature, news events, and the mechanized environment. The first—man as a creative collaborator with the machine—is best exemplified in Antoine de Saint-Exupéry, quoted earlier. Saint-Exupéry believed that the machine was a great asset to man in exploring his own nature and the nature of the world about him. "The machine which at first blush seems a means of isolating man from nature," he wrote, "actually plunges him more deeply into it." He spoke, of course, primarily of the airplane—and of the simgle prop planes which he flew. Significantly, Saint-Exupéry did not live to see or comment on Hiroshima or the Boeing 707 jets which now fill the skies. A romanticist of the machine, Saint-Exupéry nonetheless saw that the machine could humanize man, could return him to the elements from which it had so brutally severed him.

The second image fostered in popular literature is found more frequently: man as a slave to his machines. A familiar theme in fantasy and science fiction literature, man's loss of freedom—and often, life—by the product of his own hands has a chilling ring of truth to it. In Capek's *R.U.R.* the robots became eventual masters of the men who had designed them; the play ends with an appropriate, if grotesque, scene with only two characters: a robot Adam, a robot Eve.

Significantly, neither of these popular images of the man-machine gestalt—the romantic or the nihilistic—has been a major theme in the popular imagination of the twentieth century. The third image has: man as collaborator with the machine in acts of corruption, deceit, and destruction. Especially since World War II and its creation of the mechanized Golem, nuclear weaponry, the movies, television, and popular literature have portrayed a variety of possible ways in which men could utilize machines as a way of gaining advantage over other men. The James Bond novels, with their celebrated gimmickry, may have been highly popular largely for the ironic image of man they described. Strong and powerful, Bond is equipped with all the human capacities necessary for a resourceful agent and lover; but he needs and relies on the fantastic arsenal of devices as well. To be a potent human and adversary, the James Bond novels seem to say, the gimmicks are necessary. Bond is not simply a human being; he is part of a larger gestalt—fictionalized, certainly, and existing only in the extremities of superspy fiction, but nonetheless a remarkably faithful image of the man-machine gestalt.

A highly popular television show, *Mission: Impossible,* has gone beyond the Bond novels in depicting the nature of the new gestalt. The Impossible Mission Force members are high-precision espionage agents, like Bond, but lack Bond's taste for violence, and they work as a smoothly functioning team to pull unseen coups that Bond could never have managed. Viewing *Mission: Impossible* is less like seeing a tense spy drama than watching the workings of a fascinating assembly line. A substantial amount of the program is spent on mechanics—the brilliant engineer Barney Collier rigging a car to drive automatically from a remote-control operator or setting a computer to play a critical chess game. In the process of the show, the team's plan dominates everything that happens; the reactions of adversaries are anticipated and made to fit into the plan—and at every step, in almost every aspect, mechanical gadgets serve as highly efficient, precise assistants. Even the scale of the program—its concentration on the range of image—is fitted to the machines.

The image of man which emerges from the Bond novels and the *Mission: Impossible* series is subtle, though all that more effective. Here the gestalt becomes a being capable of deceiving and overcoming others; its power works subtly, quietly, but potently.

Admittedly, the man-machine gestalt has operated in many beneficial and positive ways for men, but its depiction in the media and the popular imagination has emphasized its capacities for conquering others, not specifically benefiting them. As a result, the image of the man-machine gestalt as a destructive agency is stronger than the image of it as a creative agency.

The third major consequence of the man-machine gestalt in-

volves a new sensibility toward power. In the chapter on automobiles it was suggested that men depend on automobiles to
satisfy an urge for the expression of power denied them by an
overly organized, technological civilization. The power in an
automobile becomes a source of personal power—as the town
meeting or one's craft had been in the past.

But the new sensibility toward power involves more than
this shift to a dependence on the machine for an experience of
wielding personal power. Technology distances man from the
power which he wields; yet there are forms of machines in
which the ratio between man and the power he feels has been
kept high; the motorcycle is a major example. In the new sensibility toward power, as with other consequences, the man-
machine gestalt has bred ambivalent results.

The new sensibility toward power can be seen in both poles: a
state of habituation toward larger and more vital forms of power
at the other end of a button, so that they are expected, and in a
sense, needed; and an almost contradictory desire to *feel* and experience the throb and vitality of whatever power is expended.
In both cases the expectation for increased power exists; only
the distance between man and the expended power differs.

The desire for greater power without a sense of personal involvement can be seen vividly in advertising for many consumer
products—from high-powered luxury cars (with their enticing
descriptions of comfort interwoven with almost frightening data
on horsepower) to lawn mowers that promise more in the way
of a gentle ride and suntan than well-clipped grass. As a consequence of the man-machine interface, this uninvolving attitude
toward increased power makes sense; the more the machine can
do, the less man has to do. It is almost a way of being able to
avoid the interface while at the same time taking advantage of it.

At the other end of the pole, a desire for breaking down the distance between the operator of a machine and the power which it exerts acts in two ways: as a reaction to the middle-class usurpation of machine power without sensitivity or involvement, and likewise as a genuine desire to experience the man-machine interface in its most vital form.

Custom and sports cars have always been a part of this reaction; but neither breaks down the insulation as does the motorcycle. The motorcycle may be the classic example of the totally involved man-machine gestalt.

The following was transcribed from discussions with motorcycle drivers:

> There is nothing more *machinery* than a motorcycle . . . it's *all there*, there's nothing covered up; the engine's doing engine things right there. There is an intimate contact between man and machine; there aren't any plush seats, or pedals to push or all this yadiyada. If you want to shift gears you put your foot in the transmission and kick them around, you know. . . . mechanized travel in a car is really sort of *degrading*. Man, you're surrounded with a plastic reality, it's a total unreality . . . there's a curve-around tinted glass between you and the world, and like all the little padded trinkets reassure you that you're not out in the world, or anything. It closes and you have the very solid *thunk* of the door to encapsulate you. *I* get a very perverse satisfaction in driving a bike through the rain for hours and hours on end . . . absolutely soaked, cold, exhausted, chills; there's a satisfaction to it, same way there must have been riding a horse.*

Many have found the motorcycle cults hard to explain. Our interfaces, particularly the man-machine gestalt, have been so insulated, so designed for maximum comfort, that the real power

* Henry S. Stone, "Youth and Motorcycles," in Gyorgy Kepes, ed., *The Man-Made Object* (New York: Braziller, 1966), pp. 179–180.

and vitality of an interface is lost. Motorcyclists, perhaps more than anyone else, have retained a healthy sense of the power which can not only be exerted but *felt* in the man-machine gestalt.

Both poles—toward greater power and greater insulation, and toward greater power and decreasing insulation—point to the new sensibility the man-machine gestalt has engendered: a desire for increased power at one's fingertips, with the concomitant conviction that this power is a strictly personal thing, involving few social responsibilities. Consequently, the power in the man-machine ratio rises constantly, while little or nothing is done to explore the social significance of the interaction of the new, increasingly powerful gestalts, whether on the road, over a network, or in an automated factory.

The capacity for man to grow as a human being via the interfaces is largely the capacity to relate wholly to the power in the machines he encounters so frequently in a technological environment. If power becomes no more than a way of aggrandizing oneself—the well-hidden, barely heard engine of the Cadillac—then theorists like Ellul may be right in their prediction that man s technologies will one day destroy him, in some way or other. If, on the other hand, consciousness and conscience can coalesce in the effort to assess and guide the interface with the machine, the man-machine gestalt—unlike the Centaur—may be an image of which men can be rightly proud.

7

The Dreams That Stuff Is Made Of

THE MOVIES

> Though it has been so stupidly misused, the motion picture nevertheless announces itself as a major form of the neotechnic phase of human progress. Through the machine, we have new possibilities of understanding the world we have helped to create.
>
> Lewis Mumford*

In terms of experience, the movie may be the most potent form of environment the twentieth century has consciously felt. Perceptually, its power lies in its being a total environmental submersion, suspending all senses except those which are stimulated by projector and film. Television may well knead sensibilities and attitudes more strongly than the movies shown in theaters, but television—even color television—has not yet filled the visual field with cinemascopic color, maybe on half a dozen screens at once. Perhaps television never will.

Like the automobile, the movie is a specifically twentieth-century phenomenon. Pioneers like Lumière and Méliès were showing nickelodeon shorts in the late 1890's, but these—with

* *Technics and Civilization* (New York: Harcourt, Brace and World, 1963), p. 343.

66

the simple reproduction of the movement in a train or a sprinting horse—were more of a preface than a beginning. The first decade of the twentieth century marked the real origin of the cinema, with its experimentation in editing and its attempt to tell a story through the camera, not totally through the action. D. W. Griffith, the most inventive and important of the early pioneers, showed that a strong film was less one continuous action than a well-organized collection of fragments: a close-up of one face, a close-up of another face, a reestablishing shot that showed the whole set and all the characters.

Movies followed the twentieth century, just as the twentieth century followed the movies. While radio and television would appear later, the film prepared people for both: it broke through a journalistic hegemony of words by depicting the First World War and the events of the twenties and thirties in newsreel. It broke away from an actor-dominated drama to a dramatic style in which camera, setting, and actors contribute equally to a synergetic whole.

Our comments about the movies will concentrate on the way in which movies affect people as an environment, as a total sensorial atmosphere impinging on the senses in unique ways. The themes which films have used, the ways in which their plots and characters have contributed to the dream life of the twentieth century, will not be treated here; as an art, or as a communications medium, the film deserves a much lengthier discussion than can be afforded in this work.

Considering the film as an environment, however, the man-film interface suggests several ways in which film may be shaping major attitudes and sensibilities.

The first of these is the viewer's reaction to mobility of perspective. In a movie the camera is capable of viewing the action from the most effective viewpoint. If a man is falling off a bridge, we don't necessarily watch him from the shore, but can see him from the bridge or perhaps from the water, maybe even fall down with him. Cameras have been strapped to the sides of racing cars and to the tops of dogs' heads; they can go, literally, where people can't. Even more significant is the innate mobility given the camera by editing. The viewer does not watch everything at a static distance, whether thirty feet or four feet. In a good film, he will see almost every shot from the angle and distance that best reveals what is happening in that shot.

Mobility of perspective is a dangerous thing to get used to. The eyes begin to expect that advantage of seeing things from expressive distances. Space, you begin to recognize, tells. Experiences of fixed and especially distant spaces such as the pulpit or the classroom alienate by those same ways—a gathered group, a single figure, depending on verbal strength, may have held people in the past: no more.

By appropriating various distances and angles, the camera can concentrate on physical characteristics of people rather than depend on the traditional dramatic device of speech. The close-up is as indigenous and vital to film as the mobility of shots which gives the close-up a meaningful context. In the close-up, a character does not reveal himself so much as he permits the camera to reveal him: a facial grimace, a smile nullified by eyes blazing with rage, a fist tightened around an object—low-key expressions like this are the essence of the close-up. Speech is surely a strong aspect of the movies, but in a good film the speech will often run counter to the expressions on a face, in an eye; and the viewer always knows which is the more honest.

Bela Belasz, a European film critic, has claimed that the use of facial expression in films takes the viewer much further than speech does into the psychological reality of the film:

Facial expression is the most subjective manifestation of man, more subjective even than speech, for vocabulary and grammar are subject to more or less universally valid rules and conventions, while the play of figures . . . is a manifestation not governed by objective canons even though it is largely a matter of imitation. This most subjective and individual of human manifestations is rendered objective in the close-up.*

The effects of exposure to a medium which can concentrate so well on the face are difficult to judge. Surely one of these effects is a breakthrough of the subjective over the nonsubjective in people. We are able to identify with movie characters more quickly and more intimately than dramatic characters because we get to know their faces. The "star" system, a phenomenon created by Hollywood, suggests how much people have identified with movie characters. Humphrey Bogart and Paul Newman have become the staple of millions of dream lives, of both men and women.

The major effect again, though, has been in creating expectations. People want to discover others through their faces, through the range of nonverbal expressions, tones, even the way people walk. Movies have helped awaken the sense, dormant perhaps since the development of precise language, of communication that doesn't depend on words. The barrier between who a person is and what he says has been eroded. "Show me" is beginning to subvert "Tell me."

Both mobility of perspective and the range of nonverbal expressions promoted by movies are visual. But movies, at least since the introduction of sound in the late twenties, are not solely visual; it can be argued whether they are "primarily

---

* *Theory of the Film* (London: Denis Dobson, Ltd., n.d.), p. 60.

visual." A strong movie will integrate sound and visual image in such a way that a synergetic complication will result. For example, David Wolper's documentary *Let My People Go* follows the struggles of the Jews to establish their own independent nation between 1920 and 1947. Throughout the film the images come from newsreels and still photographs of the period: treatment of the Jews, attempts to retreat from Europe, the inability to enter Israel once it is reached, the confinement to prison camps on Cyprus after the war. While the audience sees Jews suffering and struggling to reach a land they can call their own, it hears their songs—mostly in Hebrew—the tormented and jubilant songs that have helped weld a people for centuries by keeping alive a gleam of hope. The newsreel footage is potent; the commentary, brisk and vivid, is enlightening; but the music adds the final commentary, a deeper sense of what the struggle is all about than the film footage or commentary provide together.

A movie is visual only in the sense that a comic strip is visual; the full communication in either form is impossible "without the word," without, that is, the integration somewhere, somehow, of language and the suggestion of sounds.

Even during the prime years of the silent film, when masters like Chaplin and Keaton dominated the screen, everyone was anxious for the addition of sound. It would be more like life, they believed. True, but the real power in film's coexpressiveness lies more in its ability to explore the differences in visual and audio, as well as the ways of integrating them into a single experience.

Another instance of the man-film interface comes from film's use of physical setting. Because the camera has virtually unlimited mobility, it can depict people in terms of their surround-

ings. Again, the desire for this and the purpose of this was originally a desire for realism. It is easier to identify with a story,
easier to settle into a fantasy, when the objects and places have
a ring of familiarity about them. But often what begins as a
premise for realism leads to unsuspected artistic possibilities and
unexpected effects. The use of realistic settings is a fine example
of this.

Robert Wise's horror film *The Haunting* revolves around a
house. A most haunted house, to be sure: at night floors creak
and unseen fists pound on closed doors. The house stands in a
kind of ugly monumentality away from civilization; the characters who inhabit it for the duration of the film hardly feel at
home there—except for one, a lonely woman whom nobody has
ever wanted. The real drama in the film exists between the
house and the girl, Eleanor. Eleanor gives herself to the house
in a grotesque, pseudosexual surrender; then, not much later,
the house claims her as its own by killing her, enabling her
spirit to be united with the house forever.

The role of environment is exaggerated in *The Haunting*,
but all films incorporate to some extent physical object and en-
virons within the total drama. Whether a Welsh countryside
or a bank vault surrounds the characters in a scene matters substantially in the way that a film communicates; no setting in a
movie is inherently neutral.

Indeed, films have served to explore the relative meanings
of environments, suggesting what the Welsh countryside as an
environment means for the people surrounded by it. Jean-Luc
Godard's *Alphaville*, with its chilling rectangular shapes, a
world of computers and straight lines; Michelangelo Antonioni's
L'Avventura, with the grim, lifeless rocks on the island; Hitchcock's ironic setting of the UN building in *North by Northwest*

for an international murder—such settings evoke the psychological atmosphere of the characters or situations and at the same time comment on them.

The prevalent awareness of environment as an impinging force in life has come partly from psychologists and sociologists; but perhaps it has come more strongly, and more deeply, from the experience of films, in which environments are such an organic aspect of the whole. Just as films educate a sensitivity to facial expression, they stimulate an awareness of environment and an ability to recognize in various environments the distillation of human attitudes, feelings, and relationships.

Another consequence of the man-film interface in environment is the slow growth of an image of man as an environmental creature. Man is shaped by and shapes his environment; indeed, this is a key method of evolution for man. A ghetto is frightening because finally people are beginning to realize that it is not simply a place but the externalization of a condition which they have too long ignored. Man is gradually being seen as being part of a gestalt, rather than a gestalt in himself; and the total gestalt is revealed in film as nowhere else.

These four instances of the man-film interface are only a few aspects of the total effects of the interplay betwen man and the environment of movies. Perhaps, though, they are the most evident and theologically significant. In each of these instances the film interface is shown to affect man's perceptual world: how he sees faces, the world from a mobile perspective, and environments, and how he experiences coexpressive language, profoundly affects what he sees outside of the theater or away from the television set. Movies demand a world of movement, forms of expression other than words, a deepening awareness of environments and their significance for man.

The consequences of the man-film interface raise a number

of interesting questions for the church to consider. Mobility of perspective alone may have made preaching and many of the traditional approaches to worship obsolete. The standardized distance between a preacher and his congregation, as well as between a liturgical action and its participants, jolts the expectations nurtured by the pace and visual effectiveness of movies. It is not only that people want to see a preacher or liturgical actions from a more revealing distance; they have come to sense that their relationship to the action or preacher *depends* on the space between them. The fixed, immobile space created by most chapels and churches—and rigidly emphasized by rows of pews —is locked into a timeless, hierarchical pattern. People sensitized to the meaning of space as a way of involving them subjectively can only feel that the arthritic spatial experience in churches serves largely to separate them. Involvement, to what extent there is involvement, depends on words, maybe songs (usually, again, distant from the familiar contemporary modes). But aside from architecture, the visual experience is more deadening than enlivening.

Mobility of perspective offers a fresh challenge to not only preaching and liturgy but also to theology. Theology always assumes a perspective, a viewpoint. Generally this perspective has tended to be polarized by two distinct approaches: a revelational theology, which accepts Christ as the revealed Word of God as basis; or an anthropological theology, which begins with man's religious yearnings and experiences. The sensibility aroused by a mobility of perspective senses the inherent dangers of depending solely on one perspective. The most honest and revealing exploration of anything depends, people feel, on an agility of approach, a capacity to make nimble, tentative excursions, unhampered by dogmatic constrictions. A phenomenon —whether of faith or of experience—should best be approached through the perspective which, like that of the camera, is most revealing. To submit belief in Christ as God to rigorous text analysis of the Gospels is as dangerous and wrongly directed an attempt as trying to interpret man's relationship with the world solely in sacramental terms. Both efforts fail to recognize that perspective comes not from an insecurity of belief but rather from a more sincere desire to be honest with theological reality. Witness Bonhoeffer.

The increasing vocabulary of nonverbal expression nurtured by the man-film interface offers another promising avenue of consequences. Christianity has grown as part of the Greek-Roman culture, which Western civilization has inherited. As such, the early Christians shared many of the strengths and biases of Western culture. One of these strengths was language, the most resilient and flexible language up to that time. But a consequent bias was what cultural historian Rudolf Arnheim calls the "verbal bias," a suspicious attitude toward forms of communication which were not primarily verbal. The verbal bias can be seen in the slow growth of Western art, and even more prominently in education, in which curricula from the Roman era—and up to the twentieth century—focused heavily on the language arts (from literature and grammar to the study of foreign languages) while neglecting studies that depended on visual understanding, such as art and geography. In Christianity this bias is no less pronounced: St. John used two primary images for Christ, Word and Light. Which one has dominated both popular understanding and theological interpretation of Christ? Theology itself has been highly verbal, and although great works of art have reflected beliefs, visual art has never been considered a form of theological language.

In educating several generations to the potential of visual communication, movies have upset the verbal bias. Officially, it is still there; the schools and the churches depend on words far more than they do on methods of communication which are primarily nonverbal. But people, especially young people, no longer believe in the verbal bias; the new songs, the new dances, and the new movies depend on rhythm, a harmony of body and spirit, a visual understanding which is direct and needs no intercessory step of language. Where does this leave the churches? Where does it leave theology?

If the church exists to explore the meaning of man's existence and to suggest what meaning is, then very possibly its efforts in this exploration should accept man in terms of the nonverbal: what he says in his face, in his body, through the configurations he creates around himself, by the style of house, objects, and friends he acquires. Does a sermon have to be words? Can't it be a dance, a communion of expressions, a montage of photographs about man and where he is, who he is? Need theology be verbal? Cannot the forms available today—whether film, art, recording tape, or even the comic strip—provide means with which articulate men and women can express the realities of their lives in terms of a revealed God, and the realities of that God in terms of their lives? The potentials are staggering. But then, one strong look at the yawning chasm that we calmly call the "generation gap" suggests that the needs for such an exploration may be just as staggering.

An exploration of the nonverbal in liturgy, preaching, religious education, and theology need not be antiverbal. As far as we know, many concepts are impossible without words, especially the more abstract and complex ideas. The principle of coexpressibility offers an important guideline for pursuing nonverbal forms. If the final communication is synergetic, if it contains what neither the verbal nor the nonverbal alone can, then a coexpressive form has been used rightly. The exploration of nonverbal communication in the churches demands a heightened sensitivity to what words can do and what they cannot do. The picture of a Vietnamese woman clutching her charred, dead child speaks with a directness and a ferocity unavailable to words. You cannot find words to "fit" such a picture; you can only hope to find words which act as a catalyst between the picture and the reader, or perhaps words which make the picture itself a catalyst. Either way, the total result lies beyond picture and beyond words: in a potent, gripping interface which the movies have shown us is possible, but which the churches have heretofore ignored.

The fourth area—a developing awareness of the environmental interface itself—needs little comment. In a sense, this book has emerged from such awareness, and the consequences of this awareness are suggested in the various chapters, especially the final chapter. Man is no longer naked; he clothes himself with the products of his own technologies and begins identifying himself in terms of such clothing. The churches do not, cannot, speak to man so much as to suburban man, urban man, or rural man. We are all emperors with new clothing as McLuhan says. Even if someone likes to see us as "we really are" (whether the churches or the existentialists), we believe in that clothing, and our belief is hard to shake. What is more, we believe in others' clothing, and relate to them on the basis of it. A depressing allegory but a valid one: the older values have lost their handles, and so we cling to our environments, attempting, on the basis of this, to be sure of something. The hope is that by understanding just what we believe this new clothing to be, we can better live with it, and perhaps reach a time when we will be capable of living without it.

8

Reflections of Reflections

WHERE MEN WORK

> The internal character of a man is often expressed in his exterior appearance, even in the manner of his walking and in the sound of his voice. Likewise the hidden character of things is to a certain extent expressed in their outward forms.
>
> Paraclesus

If you stand on any one of a thousand spots in Manhattan, you can look up at one of the glass-faced buildings and see reflected in it the gleam and shape of another glass-faced building, the one across the street. And if you can look carefully enough (you have to be looking from the proper angle), you can see the first building framed in the second building's reflection—and so on, like mirrors repeating themselves ad infinitum.

Men have always thought of their tall structures as reflections of their prowess and triumph over nature: whether the pyramids, the Great Wall of China, or the Time-Life Building. So strange though, yet so appropriate, that where one walks along the bed of gigantic canyons of steel and glass, the buildings reflect most immediately not man but each other.

The interface between men in a large metropolis and the buildings which they pass daily and in which they spend many of their conscious hours is constituted in part by the reflector nature of the new architecture. This is true not only in the heart of Manhattan or Houston but on most college campuses, in most industrial complexes, almost everywhere men gather to work. Where brick once isolated and insulated the inside from the outside, perhaps for privacy, perhaps for sheer separation, glass now does the trick. But there is a profound difference: glass, unlike brick, is visually active, constantly catching the landscape around it, the other buildings, the trees and hills nearby, the mood of the sky. Inside, the drapes may be closed, and the air conditioner may be overcoming whatever heat the treated glass is letting in; but from the outside, the building stands as an almost conscious reminder of its immediate surroundings. The new buildings are too drably rectangular, too flat and spatially unimaginative, to draw much attention to anything other than their immense size; their strategy, therefore, is to provide the fascination of a mirror; to reflect what lies around them, even if this will only be more tall buildings with the design of a package of cigarettes. The beat goes on.

Norman Mailer has said that today you can't tell schools from factories from hospitals from prisons, the shapes and surfaces of the new "plants" are so much alike. Perhaps it doesn't matter to a school board that the school which children attend would remind them unconsciously of the factories where their fathers work; but it is certain to matter to those children, and to affect what happens to them in the school. Likewise, you can step onto any floor of almost any downtown office building and be unable to identify what industry or service the office represents, except for the words printed on the doors or glass. From the outside, the new architecture reflects its own kind; from inside and outside, it reflects the triumph of management over the processes and products that management serves.

The spaces in which men worked were once dominated by the kind of work they did. Fishermen lived in and out of boats, with the smell of the ocean a constant reminder that they were fishermen. Walking down a street in urban London two centuries ago, a foreigner without knowledge of the language could distinguish inns from shops, shipping offices from law offices; each place had its own kind of space and its own tone. Today even most bookstores have the look and feel of department stores, where each item is placed in full view, given the same visual value as any other item—no longer the mystery and suspense of crammed, dimly lit stacks where treasures lay snugly tight against trash.

The architectural environment no longer exists directly as much for products and services as for the human and mechanical processes which culminate in products and services. One of the most vitiating forces among students in recently built colleges is the awareness of the architecture as reminder of the impersonality of the educational organization. The buildings seem very often like imitations of an IBM processing unit: all the lines are strictly horizontal and vertical; the offices have a deadening similarity, like digital sorting devices (which they are). Even classrooms, built so much to the standard specifications of a classroom, seem like purely functional units, elements of a process which has already been programmed by distant administrators. Older classrooms, like older offices, are forgivable: they didn't know then, they didn't feel then, what we know and feel today. No, the newness of the modern design, on campus, in offices, or in factories, usually exacerbates the sense of a distance between the person and the end results of what the person is doing.

It should be said, parenthetically, that these remarks do not apply to all newer architecture; the exceptions are numerous enough, almost, not to be exceptions. And it is true that even the most banal of the new buildings contain numerous advantages over older ones: they are generally safer, enable easier communication and transportation among the people inside, and from the viewpoint of lighting and air are no doubt healthier. The problem is that on the level of sensory interface—what one sees and touches and hears—these new buildings seem almost anesthetic. Their surfaces have no texture to speak of; the lighting often covers the ceiling, illuminating everything at once and eliminating all shadows and relative darkness; the spaces are defined almost entirely by sharply rectangular shapes. A home, perhaps, to specific processes of production and marketing; but how much to the human spirit, with its penchant for shadows and gritty surfaces, its life of surviving rhythms and shapes?

What happens to people who spend their working hours in these buildings? They are surrounded by visual, auditory, and tactile reminders that they are functioning in a larger process, and that their function in the process is all, really, that counts. Some, if they are lucky, may be able to initiate their function or change it; but it remains—thanks, largely, to the place in which it happens—a function. Usually machines, more increasingly computers, serve as separate, critical elements in the process; the buildings serve as excellent reminders of this.

Two critical features of today's architecture emphasize the process that the buildings stimulate: their scale and their stylized uniformity.

Scale is a major keynote of all architecture. A building serves those who inhabit it, not only by creating and separating spaces in a convenient way but by devising those spaces to the scale of the people who use them. The scale of a 48-story, block-long building is determined not so much by the individuals who throng in and out of it daily, however, as by the organizations for which they work. The very fact that buildings are now named after organizations (Pan-Am, Time-Life, Prudential) rather than individuals or themes, as they were earlier in the century (Empire State, Wrigley, Chrysler), symbolizes the shift. This is not to say that the earlier skyscrapers were built entirely on a human (as against an organizational) scale—although with their individual windows, distinguished from the brick, and their shop-filled lobbies, they were probably closer. The new skyscrapers have, usually, naked lobbies surrounded by glass, and windows which can hardly be differentiated from the sheer glass walls of the building. The new scale is totally organizational, in the sense that whatever traces of the individual may have been left in earlier periods have disappeared; one enters a building to be confronted not with people but with an organization, and the process which that organization embodies and directs.

Scale is an essential aspect of the interface experience with modern architecture. One cannot help feeling overwhelmed by the new buildings: not, God forbid, because of their beauty or even so much their size, but for their scale: one senses vaguely that a new kind of being has come to inhabit the land of the central city and that the new buildings being erected are homes for this new being, made for its comfort and specifications.

A visit to a typical organization office illustrates this new scale vividly. You step in the door and onto the carpet of a lounge which has been carefully designed to be comfortable—but which you know cannot really be, for the organization inhabits the place. A pity: the furniture is so modern, usually quite expensive. A receptionist sits at a desk, on which there is a modern little switchboard and intercom; she asks in very pleasant tones (depending on the time of day, how pleasant) whom you wish to see. The casual visitor is refused access to the inner sanctum of the organization unless someone inside confirms his entry.

All this, of course, can be explained in terms of business etiquette or efficiency. But the larger patterns, the interface, is what is most striking: the building does not serve to protect and assist the individual as much as it does the organization. Unchecked entry threatens the process; and it is the process, finally, for which the building exists (it is the process which has purchased the building in the first place).

The second critical feature of the new architecture is its uniformity. Not only are the buildings alike from the outside; they are strikingly similar from the inside. Office buildings have never been distinguished for their experiments in uniqueness— why should they? The problem here is that recent ecological shifts have changed the meaning of the offices for those who work in them. The telephone, computer, and Xerox machine have contributed to a revolution in the patterns of working habits which make the office next door about as close or distant as an office across town or across the country. In previous decades a man could attach some significance to the little space in which he worked, whether it was a large office, a tiny office, or a spot on an assembly line. Increasingly, the possibility for this significance is vanishing. The new communications networks have become a more immediate, and in terms of the process a more important, environment in which people work. Very few executives or managers feel as strongly about the walls which surround them as they do about the telephone on their desk.

The ongoing effect here is roughly what Mircea Eliade calls a "desacralization of space." Specific spaces cease to have special meanings. The normal office—usually very transitory anyway, when people are constantly moving from one office into another

—has scant meaning of its own aside, perhaps, from the name and position painted on the door. An office becomes as irrelevant and inconsequential a place as an elevator: totally neutral, totally transitory. Yet, in its contribution to movement in the process, totally necessary.

Theologically, the effects of the modern architectural environment are threefold: a new sensibility has been awakened by the new buildings, to which the churches should respond; the identity which the buildings tend to confer needs to be challenged; finally, the new architecture has helped displace the sense of special, or sacred, places—a highly significant factor for churches, which have depended so much on a church or cathedral as a sacralized space.

The new sensibility which modern industrial and organizational architecture has nurtured is difficult to describe. Man is an aesthetic animal who tends to find beauty in almost any forms that surround him. Not beauty in the sense that he gazes for protracted times at a wall in an office or the front of a building, but in the sense that he can feel relatively comfortable amid the colors and lines of the new architectural landscape. The sensibility of equating functional form with beauty is surely not new; but its acquiescence to forms often without innate vitality or gracefulness—forms which emerge from the simplest construction demands of structural steel—marks a new aspect of this sensibility. Totally functional forms, made without any real attempts at artistic integrity—for example, the standard double-pile bridge built to span a superhighway—come to seem beautiful in their own right. Beauty may no longer reside as much in the eye of the beholder as in the convenience and effectiveness of the object.

There is a profound healthiness in this sensibility, an acknowledgment that beauty thrives on the innate nature and working of an object, not in external ornamentation. A man is beautiful when he is who he is, when what he says gibes with what he means. An organization or community such as the church can, supposedly, be beautiful and meaningful—but only when it lives truthful to its own beliefs and aspirations. It is a worn truism that youth today reject sham and false posturing; the readiness for such rejection may well run far beyond the young—the recent generation of architecture has helped to promote a mood suspicious of false fronts and more than simple ornamentation— not only among the youth but for anyone living in today's cities.

The second effect of the new architecture goes beyond the aesthetic. Each physical environment nurtures a specific mode of identity; a person tends to think of himself as being who he is in terms of the places where he lives and works. Recent industrial architecture promotes the identity of a man who serves as a unit of a whole. But his whole is not a community, not even, strictly speaking, an organization, but rather a process, an ongoing evolution of certain steps which result somewhere in a product—and for the man, in a paycheck and the constant hopes of upward movement. The man's actual relationship to the organization is enigmatic: he may depend on it, but it is questionable to what extent he trusts it. After all, the new architecture and the nature of the organization itself generally suggest a state of flux, something always in a transitory stage. The office manager or vice-president is always riding the elevator, and any floor he steps onto will only be there for him so long as the process demands.

A self-image of the individual as a shifting, though reliable, unit in a process much larger than he can control, or often even comprehend, is a major effect of the new architecture. And it is one which has great portent for theology.

Organization man is not so much an economic as a processual creature, a man caught up in processes which are dominated by the organization. In many ways this squares with a Teilhardian view of history, but in other ways it conflicts strongly with the traditional Christian interpretation of human possibilities. Architecture, only one visual reminder of the processes to which men are committed, may not be countered by so naïve an attempt as forms of church architecture which suggest a different image of man. The greatest need, perhaps, is to foster an awareness of the visual environment: what the buildings are doing, saying, to those who work in them and pass them daily. If this awareness is developed in the context of a richer sense of human lives than the buildings suggest, very possibly their influence will not be so strong—or at least it may be more conscious, and therefore more capable of stimulating conscious response.

The churches were once powerful in their ability to nurture identity, to provide an environment (not unlike the architectural environment of today's cities) in which men could reach self-images through their identification with it. Today the church, at least in America, possesses no strong environment: its power, if there is to be any, must seek a different shape. The challenge posed by the new architecture is fundamentally a challenge to consciousness. It suggests that the new education consists in awakening people to environments rather than circumscribing their minds with new, doctrinal environments. Environments needn't, like fires, be fought always by other environments; often an alert consciousness may be a far better weapon.

Indeed, the question of church architecture as an environment might well be posed here. A church, especially one with simple, striking design, may well be an environment that encourages prayer and stimulates a psychological openness to worship. But as noted above, one of the effects of the new architecture has been the desacralization of space. And not only office space but all space; the very possibility of a special place being set aside for its magical portents, its saving possibilities, or even its sentimental value has been seriously diminished. One factor has been the gradual secularization process at work so profoundly in our culture the last few hundred years. But perhaps another, even more potent, factor may be the character of the pervasive new environments: television, radio, computer, and telephone are not ground to place; they are not even, in the perceptual interfaces they stimulate, primarily spatial. In a world of electronics and instant communication, place diminishes and becomes irrelevant as an environment. Consequently, the meaning of a special space or place, set aside and suggesting a meaning by the very fact it *is* set aside, becomes less and less significant.

The church, ever since it has emerged from the catacombs, has bound itself to specific buildings, specific spaces; it has tended, subsequently, to identify itself in terms of these bonds. (The very word "church" has the sometimes confusing but illustrative double meaning of community of believers and actual building.) The most striking reminders of the "age of faith" are the enormous cathedrals its people erected. Most people knew the church from going to church, from their experience with altar, pulpit, confessional. What is the future of church buildings—what is the future of the identification process between the Christian and his church—in an age in which electronic technology is usurping the sacral sense of space?

The immediate reaction, of course, is to conserve church buildings as a last rampart against the desacralization of space. Here, at least, is one place, one island in the city, where man can step aside for silence, for moments with God, for communion. This is true; but if the churches do not at the same time offer a way in which those sensibilities nurtured by the electronic environment can likewise relate to God and to other men in a Christian context, the churches will be doing little more than preserving a remnant of the past—until it atrophies into its inevitable oblivion.

Experiments in liturgical services which do not depend on a specific plan—services in offices, apartments, public parks, and coffeehouses—may be one possible avenue. The use of church buildings themselves for activities other than explicit prayer and worship may be another. The important thing is to explore the relation of the church, so long anchored to the churches crowned with spires and crosses, to a world in which the church building has ceased to have its earlier, psychological meaning.

The interface with contemporary architecture may seem to be one of the least conscious and most unintentional of the new interfaces. Yet, for that matter, it may be all the more significant. The eyes and ears record more than any man can retain awareness of, much less give thought to. And if these impressions, over a time, tend to form some kind of a gestalt, are they to be ignored, simply because they have not been rendered totally conscious? It is the same with rock songs on radio, television commercials, and the voice over a phone: more is gathered than is garnered. And who is to say what becomes of the surplus?

9

The Sound and the Flurry

TODAY'S AURAL ENVIRONMENT

> If we sit and talk in a dark room, words suddenly acquire new meanings and different textures. They become richer, even, than architecture, which Le Corbusier rightly says can best be felt at night. All these gestural qualities that the printed page strips from language come back in the dark, and on the radio. Given only the *sound* of a play, we have to fill in *all* of the senses, not just the sight of the action.
>
> Marshall McLuhan*

Unlike many other environments spawned by technology, the sound environment is, practically speaking, inescapable. It is a drastically new acoustical world we encounter: the natural sounds of wind, birds, and the quiet hum of village activity that filled the air before the industrial era may not have disappeared, but they have been swallowed up into the cacophony of screeching brakes, trucks in first gear, and passing airplanes.

No one knows what the persistence and high level of undesired noise is doing to our ears or to our selves. A recent study in *Scientific American* shows that the decibel level in large

* *Understanding Media: The Extensions of Man* (New York: McGraw-Hill Book Company, 1964), p. 303.

cities has reached a danger zone—a threshold beyond which the ears are permanently damaged and the individual is subjected to a kind of aural abrasion which can be more potent and wearing than physical abrasion.

Sound works on man in a fundamentally different way from the operation of vision. Sight has an objectivity about it; spaces are coherent and interrelated; the fall of light and projection of shadow, the mixture of colors, and the proportionate sizes of things enable us to judge accurately the shape and significance of an environment. But sound works on man more subjectively. Its major functional purpose—speech—suggests this; while visual expression, such as writing, serves as an objectivization of the self, speech works simply as a relating of two subjectivities. Hearing is by far more intimate, more personal, more emotionally charged, than seeing. It is inevitable that a drastically changed sound environment will have effects on the inner person that may not be nearly so noticeable as the effects of an altered visual environment.

Modern radio, in many respects the most apparent aural environment, is largely a response to the high threshold of noise in the cities. How best kill unpleasant noise—by insulating a home or office against it or by covering it with a more pleasant, satisfying kind of noise? Certainly the blanketing of other noise is not the major function of radio today; there are many other factors. But the not uncommon need that many people have to keep a radio playing at every moment, in car and out of car, suggests that the radio acts as some kind of protection against the more unruly noises that are otherwise difficult to escape.

Noise is not an inappropriate term to describe today's radio. Noise that depends for its effect not so much upon its organization or coherence as upon its friendliness and the involvement of the sound. The disc jockeys, the frantic and soothing commercials, and the music—whether the Rolling Stones or Mantovani—contribute to a synergetic whole which is totally aural, which involves the listener less in content than in sound. Top-Forty radio, which polls show is by far the most popular radio, works because of the sound. It is not so much what is said by the jockey, the commercials, the song; it is the way in which it is said, the beat, the tempo, the fervor behind it. Radio, once a highly verbal medium, has witnessed and undergone a triumph of the nonverbal over the verbal.

"Hey, baby! This is me! Rockin' Robbie D! I'm so bad I make flowers die I make babies cry I take candy from babies and give dogs rabies and if that ain't bad the rain don't fall and that ain't all—biscuits ain't bread." And so Detroit, like other major cities, is assaulted daily; the words rush out in torrents, too fast to follow, too powerful to feel; the sense is that of being flooded, overtaken by a tempo and energy that makes use of words, just as in earlier ballads words made use of melodies.

The commercials may be just as vitalistic and overpowering— a strong, fast ditty or the disc jockey blazing through a written announcement with inconceivable speed. Some listeners might catch a few of the words, but the total effect, the synergetic whole, is something far beyond the words. One is no longer confronted with a radio commercial or a disc jockey's chatter; he is surrounded by it. Sound can work this way, and radio has made it work this way.

It is a common myth about rock radio that the records are made for kids and sold to kids, and that the DJ's and commercials aim at kids. Actually, a good share of a lively rock station's audience—and a share the DJ's aim for—is the eighteen- to thirty-four-year-old population, the young married, the rising new managers who teethed on Elvis in high school and have stayed with the movement ever since. Teen-agers may be closest to radio, they may feel more at home with it, but the rock stations no longer belong exclusively to them. Indeed, countless people feel that listening to rock radio helps keep them young—drawing from one of the major resources of the younger generation.

Teen-agers, however, play the most important role in the ritual of Top Forty. The Top Forty is a curious phenomenon, something that perhaps only radio could have spawned and managed to cope with. The difference between the new Beatles recording being number twelve or number seven might not matter a great deal to most people, but to many of the disc jockeys and to many of the listeners, it is cause for celebration when a record makes the significant "jump" from twenty-third place to fifteenth, or from fourth to second. The teens are rooting for a record (or more frequently, a group or singer, whom the record represents); they can even participate in the ritual by helping boost a record through buying it (the Top Forty is an index of record purchasing). The number one record slot has a peculiar mystique about it, even though by the time a record makes number one its repeated sound (a listener may have heard it dozens of times by then) has begun to wear. The music itself is fascinating. Few people can listen to it while sitting still. It invites—no, demands—movement, a nodding of the head at first, eventually the whole body. And not just the teens: young housewives don't move listlessly through their chores to the sound of the new rock groups so much as they perform these tasks with a repertoire of familiar loose gyrations that make the whole activity a kind of dance.

And the groups and singers.. The final attraction of radio does not lie so much in the pleasantness of its sound as in its power to communicate personalities in intimate, personal ways.

The Beatles, Donovan, the Vanilla Fudge—these are not names, not simply references to accomplished rock artists; these are people who communicate with other people. The "fan craze," which became amply apparent in the days of Elvis or Paul Anka lives on, but perhaps on a slightly different premise. Up until the revolution in rock and roll, sparked when Bob Dylan turned from folk to rock, a singer's style and personal appeal were his major assets. He looked good, he sounded great, his body moved in a way that enlivened millions of schoolgirls' fantasy lives: this was enough. But the post-Dylan generation (which, significantly, contains a much larger proportion of college students than the pre-Dylan generation did) is more sophisticated; the listeners expect the singers not only to appeal to them but to communicate, and on the burning questions of their lives: love and sex, authority, freedom, making some sense out of a life over which they seem to have increasingly less control. Suddenly the lyrics begin to matter as they never did before. Themes of depth and complexity replace themes that do little more than nurture a pleasant fantasy life. The distance from "Put Your Head on My Shoulder" to Dylan's ode "My Back Pages" is more than an aesthetic one, however. The change has reshaped the nature of fan worship. Whereas once the girls screamed from a sexual fascination with a star, they now listen spellbound to the gospel according to that star, the vision of life he is sharing with them. A new style of leadership has emerged, and it may be that the vision of a pop singer becoming a national liberation figure in *Privilege* or *Wild in the Streets* may not be too distant from reality.

The post-Dylan revolution in rock-singing heroes has upset McLuhan's premise that the medium is the message. Here the message (and the word is quite correct) has reshaped the medium. Radio has become for many a new gospel, a new source from which to learn the mores and morals of a generation.

And what of the disc jockeys? Their role is critical. Not only do they provide a go-between for the singers and the audience; the good DJ's—notably those in the big cities, where large stations can afford astronomical salaries—are sometimes as important to listeners as the rock stars themselves. The "jocks," as they call one another, are not simply the cheerful disc spinners of another era; they are exuberant madmen, announcing each record with enthusiasm and a swirl of adjectives that leave you wondering what they were saying. Commercials, at least the ones they read, do not sound like the dull, pious announcements frequent in TV commercials; they are vivid, jammed with personal interjections, and they appear less a function of advertising than an exhibition of the disc jockey's vocal talents.

Disc jockeys, because they are live and fresh every day, inevitably engender relationships quite similar to those of such television personalities as Mike Douglas and Johnny Carson. Out in millions of radioland homes, housewives are able to break through the solitude and banality of their existence by tuning in. A private communion between the DJ and the housewives, teen-agers, and even some men evolves. The communion may well be more meaningful and strongly felt than any other relationships a listener has. The power of the radio medium may be, fundamentally, the power of personality—projected instantly to millions of radios. The disc jockey and the singers he plays represent not so much the triumph of noise over noise as the triumph of communicating personality over a fragmented, technological society.

The effects of radio upon listeners may not be nearly so evident as the process which created these effects. A major effect, mentioned already, is the predominance of the nonverbal over the verbal. Rock song lyrics may ring with important messages, but these messages remain bound to the sound, the rhythm and tone, in which they are projected: radio's version of coexpression. The personalities nurtured by the medium are developed through nonverbal ways. As an environment, radio surrounds a person with sound, and this sound is inhibited and compromised if too much of it is words for the sake of words.

The use of words in radio may be indicative of the use of words in future areas of mass communications. Words, in an age of immediate electronic communications, may not be able to hold their own; they may become increasingly part of larger patterns, expressions which are predominantly nonverbal, in a word, synergetic. Whereas the power of words once lay in precision, the power of the new synergetic expression will be a uniting of subjectivities, a communion of spirit and sensibilities.

10

From Cathedrals to Shopping Centers

> Upon those who step into the same rivers different and
> ever different waters flow down.
>
> Heraclitus

In the Middle Ages the great cathedrals built throughout Europe served as more than architectural monuments to faith. Built near the centers of cities, they became the centers of cities. "In the main," writes Lewis Mumford, "the great church is center to the town, in every sense but a geometric one." But geometry has always played little more than an incidental role in determining patterns of human ecology "One must think of the church," continues Mumford, "indeed, as one would now think of a 'community center': not too holy to serve as a dining hall for a great festival, as a theater for a religious play, as a forum where the scholars in church schools might stage oratorical and learned disputes on a holiday. . . ."

Just as the cathedral is symbolical of the faith of that era, the ecological patterns it created symbolizes many of the assumptions of the era: the profound interaction between sacred and secular, the hierarchical status of the church over the market-place, the ability of the church to embody all of life.

In the thirteenth and fourteenth centuries, the supermarkets of that day were part of larger structures, the cathedral squares. Wedged against the squares, sometimes even into the squares, farmers and merchants sold or traded their wares. Today the supermarket is again part of a larger structure, the shopping center, heir to the ecological dominance of the cathedrals.

Like the cathedral, the shopping center symbolizes and creates its period. In an age bereft of hierarchies, no single buildings or structures dominate the shopping center—save perhaps occasional department stores or the giant symbol announcing the shopping center. Many of the newer centers have come to include, in addition to banks, post office, theaters, and restaurants, such attractions as skating rinks and an open auditorium, for club meetings or local plays. Fashion shows or car displays proliferate, sometimes in the main plaza of the new indoor centers.

The shopping center is the child of an automobile culture and a suburban populace. Its future is probably even more glorious and promising than its brief, explosive past. Shopping centers account for about 40 percent of retail sales, and experts forecast that four-fifths of America's fresh retail space will be located in the centers. As vast suburban tracts spread out from unsightly urban ghettos, geometric centers will become impossible; the new focal points will be those meccas of the modern consumer—the shopping centers.

In the shopping center the shift from the centrality and eminence of the cathedral to a large mall with shops and stores suggests a major shift in the fundamental conscious purposes of human society. To say glibly that we have moved from "sacred" to "secular" or from a religious to an economic culture does not get at the roots of the shift. The shopping center grows out of the whole complex of new media and new communications; the TV commercial and the common expectations of suburban living both contribute to the vitality and social significance of shopping centers.

Indeed, more than any other single phenomenon the shopping center symbolizes the new ecology—the patterns men in a technological society have established with their environment. Ecological patterns tend to create and symbolize changes in deeper, less perceptible patterns, as the shopping center has affected purchasing habits, the community life of suburbia, and the sense of consumer identity.

Another major symbol of the new ecology, the system of roads in America, with freeways linking cities and becoming complex entanglements like nerve synapses as they touch one another, affects more than travel. Such a system tends, eventually, to make driving something of a maze-exploring effort, involving different efforts and a different consciousness from normal city driving.

In a sense, all the subjects treated in this book—from automobiles to computers—represent aspects of human ecology, the interrelationships between man and his environment. This chapter will concentrate, however, on patterns of mobility, where things are located, how men move from one point to another and for what reasons.

It would be foolish, however, to think that the new patterns of mobility can be studied simply from a city or state map. Contemporary mobility—the change from rooted forms to more evanescent, fluctuating forms—doesn't apply only to people. Credit cards and important business meetings over a telephone likewise represent the new mobility.

The most startling feature of the new ecology is precisely its almost unlimited mobility. The spatial confines which once dominated our concepts of human presence and money are fast disappearing. A person is present over a telephone; most financial transactions no longer involve the presence of actual coins or currency. The very nature of a city as self-contained community is being broken down by interlinking subways and superhighways. The East Coast, from New York to Washington, has been called a megalopolis, an "overcity"—which, indeed, it is fast becoming. The new mobility has outmoded old confines, old concepts. A "rooted" understanding of any feature of contemporary life is becoming increasingly difficult, except in the small towns and rural areas.

Such far-reaching mobility as can be found in America signifies the breakdown of earlier ideas of what mobility—or travel, or movement—was. The conception, for example, of a "journey," so pronounced a theme in Western literature and so deeply a part of our historical consciousness, simply no longer exists. A journey implies time, distance, and most of all roots. For ten years Ulysses journeyed through the Mediterranean to return to his father's home in Ithaca. His travels were punctuated by dangers and allurements; nevertheless, Ulysses struggled to arrive home. Today the journey has been replaced with the trip or the tour. Travel no longer has the romantic, dangerous quality it once had—nor does it take much more than a slight fraction of the time. Consequently, destinations tend to lose their mystery and attractiveness, and the very act of travel loses the proportions of danger, excitement, and romance it once had.

In a sense, it could be said that total mobility has robbed mobility of its earlier meanings. The image of the Christian as a pilgrim—or of the church as a pligrim community—no longer has any suggestive force. In *Pilgrim's Progress* Bunyan proposed an allegory for the Christian life; his work was to become the second Bible of an era of Protestants. Christian, the hero, moves through his journey from the City of Destruction toward Mount Zion—signifying the journey from sin through all the phases of redemption and grace. In an age when America had just been discovered and villages and towns buzzed with talk of great journeys, such an allegory conveyed more to people than an epic image of the Christian life; it had the strength of a vicarious expedition into a new world—a world which readers could themselves penetrate in their own moral lives.

With the demise of the image of the pilgrim, a popular religious orientation to the Christian faith has proved sterile. The individual Christian life—or the life of the Christian community—cannot really be perceived today as a journey, or even a movement from place to place. Baptism, confirmation, marriage, and the seeming corridor of death lose their meaning as landmarks and become, if anything, mere concentrations of a period of time—like shopping centers on a map. On an individual or community scale, the Christian life exists as a process, one which cannot be identified ahead of time or at any precise moment. Perhaps historically it can be viewed from the perspective of time, but then it refuses to submit to regular stages, revealing itself instead as an emerging pattern, interwoven with sudden events, people, and trends.

Largely for this reason, death—the destination in the journey of the Christian life—holds only the meaning of an abortive event in the life of a society. It is far more difficult to view death personally, and with fear or faith, than ever before, simply because life no longer is conceived as leading to death. The new mobility, such a potent shaper of our outlooks and emotional reactions, has done much to rob death of its mystery and alignment with personal destiny. Like birth, death "happens"; its significance is usually felt far more strongly by the community afterward than by the person himself beforehand.

Like other major environments, the new patterns of mobility tend to reshape the identity of a generation. Once the church could depend on the metaphor of a pilgrim to give people a sense of their lives, an image of the whole. Today the images of consumer, traveler, functionary, and revolutionary touch much closer to the lives of people and say something about those lives. Yet, seemingly, these images cannot contain the breadth and richness of Christian self-actualization as we have come to know it today. In a world in which the person's choices are determined by processes which he cannot control, what image can suffice?

The problem is a poignant one, and it helps explain the profound difficulty faced by anyone who tries to describe what it means to be a Christian in truly contemporary terms. Aspects of Christian life—social conscience, community living, hope—have been highlighted, but an image of the whole, something possible for earlier generations, seems impossible today.

Here, perhaps, is the most significant result of the new patterns of mobility for Christianity. Our lives are too fluid, too shaken by the explosive events and processes of contemporary existence, to lend themselves to any clear, single metaphor. The community itself has been torn apart by the new mobility; residential parishes or even industrial parishes can neither begin with nor create real communities. The problem is not that people cannot stay in one place; it goes far deeper: they do not feel that they belong to one place. Community belongs to those who belong in the community. Loyalties like this are painfully difficult to nurture in a highly mobile society.

The new mobility with its innate tendency to uproot and cast everything into fluctuation, tends to create landscapes—both physical and emotional—in which one place has little more connotative meaning than another. In the chapter on buildings it was noted that people no longer respond to a "sacred space"; a similar process is resulting from total mobility, in that people no longer respond to special places—whether landmarks of their own youth or of history. The image of a suburban sprawl stretching from seacoast to seacoast, dotted only by shopping centers and airports, might be a horrifying thought; but in a way it captures the direction and perhaps the consequences of modern mobility, in which movement—and not destination—becomes the dominating factor.

Heraclitus, the Greek philosopher quoted at the beginning of this chapter, claimed that beneath a layer of turbulent change lies a quiet persistent unity: "Upon those who step into the same rivers different and ever different waters flow down." Perhaps such a statement does not apply to the processes of major technological change, which tend, as Whitehead says, to wreck the civilizations in which they occur. But rapid, perpetual change can be a subterfuge for a deeper unity—and in the new patterns of mobility, it well may be.

It is just possible that extreme mobility—like other technological interfaces—illuminates a fresh dimension of Christian existence, even as it darkens another. The major marches in Washington during the 1960's—for civil rights, protesting the Vietnam war, and demanding effective legislation to curb poverty—created, for a few days, communities that numbered in the tens of thousands. The marchers in these demonstrations represent a generation for which the mobility to move from California to Washington suddenly is an easy and natural choice. Their roots are neither local nor regional, but grounded in the sympathy of a cause which may have national or international ambits. What is important for the formation of these new communities, and indeed this new sense of self-identity, is not where but what. The focus of their self-conception seems to be moral rather than spatial, determined by a belief rather than by norms out of their own age.

Out of the very mobility that destroyed the old roots, then, are created new roots, possibly as binding and as nourishing as the old ones—perhaps more so. For the new roots correspond to the new ecology, to the breakdown of local autonomies and local points of view.

What kind of identity, what metaphor for Christian existence, and what kind of community are then possible? The dimensions of a Christian's self-understanding are difficult enough in any era, with the need to fight the encroachments of a culture that would readily confine and control Christian vision and passion. Today the difficulties are compounded by the mobilization of the entire society, patterns of movement that destroy the centrality of any centers other than the shopping ceners.

If a new kind of Christian community is emerging through the marches, it might be said that the new community is emerging out of the fragmentation of older communities. Likewise, if a fresh sense of Christian identity comes out of commitment to a moral society, then perhaps that fragmentation of older identities such as the pilgrim is providing the basis for a new unity.

In his prison letters Dietrich Bonhoeffer spoke frequently of the fragmented existence that his generation led. "Even though our lives may be blown to bits," he wrote to his parents in 1944, "by the pressure of events as our houses are by the bombs, yet we should still have a glimpse of the way in which the whole was planned and conceived, and of what material we were building with or should have used had we lived."

"A glimpse of the whole"—this may be all that is possible, and perhaps all that is necessary, for a generation blown apart by the mobility of contemporary society. The Christian life is an exploration of possibilities, not a neat set of stages like plateaus on a quiz contest; to explore those possibilities in terms of the situations, the challenges, and the moods of each decade is far more important than the futile effort to sink roots in sand or to build a community out of a transient populace. The age of metaphors, with their static, assuring quality, is gone; and so is the age of wholly localized communities. The only way Christians can keep movement from becoming neurotic flight, and the shopping centers from becoming the only valid centers of activity, is to find in the larger scale of moral concern a fresh community, and in the awakening awareness of our precarious world a fresh identity: out of the fragments a new whole, a new sense of unity.

11

Where Sublime and Ridiculous Converge

COMMERCIAL TELEVISION

> Anacin commercials give me a headache—an Excedrin headache.
>
> Graffiti

The most telling moments in television are often the least consciously intended ones. One evening on a national news show, a report was presented on starvation among children in Latin America. The difficulty, explained a newsman, lay less in the amount of food than in its lack of nutritional strength. Then, suddenly, the commercial had begun—a commercial for a high-cost, especially nutritious dog food. On a color set, the commercial was a powerful affront to the brief report that had preceded it. While the image of the thin, fibrous beans and crumbly bread in cracked bowls was still in viewers' minds, the camera closed in on red, meaty chunks covered with thick gravy. The viewer was left not only with a fresh shock that his shaggy terrier was eating better than millions of people on the same hemisphere but with the vague intimation that television, his society, and he himself *cared* more about the terrier than about the people.

Moments like this, in which television serves as revelation

rather than reverberation, are rare. Yet they suggest the enormous proportions of a twenty-three-inch screen—where everyday reality and fantasy are constantly intermixed. Not only does television touch more than sixty million people every day as no other medium can, not only does it touch most of them in the sanctuary of their own homes, but also television contains the power to engage, inform, delight, and disturb people. Television's presence in a home is more than a means of immediate, pleasant entertainment, it is a symbol of the power and ambience of communications in America.

The significance of the television phenomenon for Christianity in coming decades can hardly be pursued thoroughly in a brief chapter such as this. Indeed, there are so many directions to take in pursuing the meaning of television—the commercials, the stars, the content and assumptions of the shows, the expectations and moral certitudes nurtured by the series shows and the genres—that the subject surely deserves a much lengthier treatment. However, to suggest the implications of the television interface in the context of other environments, this chapter will focus on four aspects of the TV interface—what appear to be major structures of the interface. Each of these structures has considerable implications for Christianity today and in the near future.

The first of these structures is the tension in television between reality and fantasy. Nowhere else does contemporary man have to switch mental and emotional gears so quickly and so frequently in assessing the real or unreal nature of what he is seeing. A news report is followed by an extravagant spy show, which is itself followed by a pseudorealistic soap opera Western. Each show makes its own special demands on the viewer's credibility, and indeed, these demands are seminal to the effect and appeal of the shows.

But the gear-switching doesn't merely have to operate in

half-hour or hour-long segments; the incessant breaks of commercials aggravate the problem considerably. Especially considering the nature of the television commercial, which itself is usually a subtle configuration of reality (the product's advantage, the need that people in the commercial and in the audience have for it) and fantasy (the content and approach of the commercial itself—quite frequently absurd or comic). Television viewers, especially young ones, become, admittedly, adept at switching gears and accepting the real or illusory basis of what they are seeing—but in doing so, they have gone through a change in perceptual and imaginative patterns which only an age of television could have catalyzed.

The difference in perceiving the real and unreal between today's television viewers and the readers, say, of pulp fiction thirty years ago is quite a significant one. A pulp novel (or a play, or a movie) operates on a steady level of sustained fantasy. But there is no sudden break within the medium from fantasy to reality, or major jumps in the levels of fantasy and reality. Mental gear-switching can take place at a more sustained, leisurely pace. Television viewers, however, are constantly forced to accept fresh levels of fantasy and reality. So much so that over a period of such immediate adjustment, their sensibilities to fantasy and reality may tend to overlap. They begin to find in fantasy kinds of reality which may not be apparent to the "illiterate" TV viewer. Mr. Spock in *Star Trek* has had this kind of reality for many viewers. Likewise, the television viewer finds in realistic portrayals—a report, for example, on city riots— elements of fantasy which he can easily refuse to accept as totally real. The TV screen does not distort so much by its size as by its juxtaposition of radically differing contents.

The second significant structure about television lies within the television commercial itself—the single form to which any viewer is most exposed. The history of television commercials suggests that Madison Avenue has been more successful in evolving sophisticated and experimental television than have the networks. The older "hard sell" commercials—with their sledge-hammer sales pitches, or the "beat Brand X" demonstrations—are gone, with the exceptions of some soap and pharmaceutical ads. The new approaches are far more subtle, and probably much more effective; the commercial becomes a drama scaled to the interface between man and product. For example, one Gaines Gravy Train dog food commercial opens with a West-ern bandit robbing a bank. He shoots the sheriff, but the lawman's last effort is to signal his Rin Tin Tin-looking dog after the fleeing bandit. The announcer's voice cuts over the action, "Who knows what greatness lies in the heart of a dog?" As the chase goes on, with the terrified bandit spurring his horse from the sight of the large, racing German shepherd, cuts are made to a fat little pooch in a modern kitchen, chomping away at his Gravy Train. Finally the sheriff's dog jumps the bandit and sits triumphantly atop him; cut to the kitchen pooch, who barks twice, the vocal symbol of Rin Tin Tin.

A commercial such as this operates on several levels. On one level, it is a capsulized Western chase with the dog as hero; on another level, it is a tribute to the dream life of dogs and their owners ("Who knows what greatness lies in the heart of a dog?"); on yet another level, it is a drama in which Gravy Train is the hero, and the boredom and drabness of pooch's daily existence is the villain. It is, of course, on the third level that Gaines hope to (and probably will) sell dog food.

It is also on this third level—where the product itself serves as the hero—that commercials are sensitizing a generation of television viewers to the dramatic meanings of cars, aspirins, cigarettes. A Camaro is no longer simply an expensive symbol of youth and vitality; in one of its commercials, the Camaro has the presence and dramatic appeal of a movie star. The appeal of a Camaro is not so much the appeal of a bright, dynamic form of transportation as the appeal of a fascinating presence— what a Bogart or a Marlene Dietrich was to the screen a generation ago.

One of the consequences of this new approach by commercials is the tendency of the viewer to look upon these products in a less pragmatic, functional way—less, even, in terms of the status they symbolize—and to regard them more as companions, with a fascination dramatized in their commercials. The Camaro, the hundred-millimeter cigarette, the Alka-Seltzer tablets, are no longer simply things we use, but things we *like:* we are more comfortable with them around. Their presence (and not so much their functions) have been absorbed into our own lives in a way impossible before the television commercial.

A third structural effect of television can be found in the nature and approach of the series show. Newspapers and magazines have space to fill; television and radio have time to fill— and the pressure to keep the screen or radio speaker alive is far more powerful, as anyone in the broadcasting industry will readily admit, than the pressure to fill pages. In television the problem is especially acute, and the series show was created as an attempt to handle that problem.

The series show has, of course, its origins in older forms: popular fiction series, in which a basic hero followed consistent patterns over a series of episodes; and radio series, the early fore-runners of the TV series. The television series has, however, gone beyond any of its predecessors in that it forms the backbone of the medium. While prime-time television does present movies, variety and news shows and specials, the fact remains that the series—with its predictable pattern, stars, and style— dominate.

TV series are built on the psychology of expectation. That is, people tend to choose something which they have already experienced and liked. To see one *Bonanza* may be to have seen them all; but psychologically for a mass audience, seeing one is the necessary prefix for seeing them all. This is why television writers must be highly careful in working on a series to keep many factors consistent—and yet allow a fairly extensive variety each week. The constant elements suggest the basis of these expectations: the hero or heroes never really change, though they may be submitted to experiences which conceivably could change other people; the style (pace, music, language, points of emphasis—say, facial expressions or gadgetry) remains constant; the way in which the plot develops and is resolved stays pretty much the same. What then changes? The other people, the precise nature of the challenge, the specific responses required of the hero—certainly not as much, though, as remains unaltered.

The effect of the series on a TV viewer may well be a strong one. What happens to a man who can make most of his choices on a television screen on the basis of highly reliable expectations? He knows what he is about to see, and that is why he chooses to see it. Very possibly, his sense of expectation is deeply affected by this: he tends to prefer expectations in which he is thoroughly familiar with what is to come. Innate human conservativism? Perhaps partially. Largely, though, an education conferred by the TV series.

The fourth structural effect of television is so nebulous as almost to defy description. In *The Mechanical Bride* McLuhan attempted to get at the way in which some advertising campaigns in the late 1940's were shaping consciousness. An advertisement for ladies' stockings, for example, would depict only a pair of legs: very sexy legs, assuredly, but only the legs. McLuhan hypothesized that the proliferation of ads like this did something to the national consciousness of sex, that people felt and thought a little differently about sex as a result of seeing those legs, that sex not only had an appeal through pure anatomy but an appeal through segregated *parts* of the anatomy. "Notice any very spare parts lately?" he quipped. But the question had its heavier side: in a machine age, when everything from electric shavers to Boeing jets can be dissembled and reassembled, how do we look upon sex and the body?

Television, both in its shows and in its commercials, is far more powerful than magazine advertising ever was. How is it affecting the consciousness of those who watch it, especially the young? The Saturday morning cartoons, with their superheroes pitted against maniacal villains, the fate of the world hanging precariously in the balance; the soap operas, in which infidelities and undesired pregnancies serve as the moral basis for drama; the situation comedies, which reduce their characters to such levels of patent stupidity that the audience is incapable of laughing with them and can only laugh at them—what do shows like these do to the consciousness of their viewers?

This fourth consequence of the television interface—a subtle, inelectable shaping of consciousness—is really impossible to describe except in terms of specific shows and specific commercials. Nonetheless, given the visual power of the screen itself, its presence in the home and the number of hours it is watched, it is hard to believe that our attitudes toward life, drama, sex, and the world about us are not really affected.

There are, of course, more than these four consequences. These—the sharpened distinction between reality and fantasy, the growing sense of the product as star, the training process of expectations, and the subtle shaping of consciousness—have been emphasized because they seem to be strategic areas in the television interface, strategic in that they all hold key significance for the caliber of religious life in the future.

All of these effects, it should be noted, move from content to sensibility. We are not affected by the content in a direct, overwhelming way (as berated citizens often protest nudity or excessive violence in films and TV); we are affected by the way in which the content reaches us over a sustained period of time. For the most powerful single thing television has going for it *is* time. Nielsen estimates that during January and February of 1968 the average American family watched 46 hours, 32 minutes a week. That's upwards of six hours a day. A lot of television.

It is presumptuous, no doubt, and early to estimate the total significance of television for the quality of man's religious life, but these four effects help to cast a little light. The first, the powerful interplay between fantasy and reality, may contain the clearest implications for religious awareness. Christianity, like other religions, has always contained a tension between fantasy and reality in its own myths and beliefs. Only in the twentieth century, with the firm attempt to "demythologize" religion, have real attempts been made to segregate the two elements. Christians have begun to realize that Jonah's three days in the whale didn't necessarily have the same degree of historical reality as Christ's days in the tomb. Indeed, Christ's death and resurrection as described in the Gospels needn't be so absolutely historically accurate as earlier generations thought. Mythological truth can be more powerful—and in a way more truthful—than historical truth; or putting it another way, fantasy can say more about reality than historical reality itself can.

Television has educated millions of people to a sensitivity for the expressive potential of fantasy as well as to the expressive potential of realism. Not only a sensitivity, however: an ability as well to adjust to either fantasy or realism immediately. This means that people who once might have accepted the mythological and the historical on the same level will now be more sophisticated, more discerning in understanding their beliefs. It is imperative that mythical elements of the Old and New Testaments, if they be taught and interpreted, be taught and interpreted as myths—as elaborate religious fantasies created to enrich and sustain belief. Whatever is solidly historical in the Bible needs likewise to be understood as being validly historical. But any attempt to reduce the two levels to one level would be a grave mistake; the audience accustomed to television can discriminate too well, too quickly.

The challenge posed to Christianity by this first effect of television is hardly one of better biblical studies or even better understanding of the Bible as much as a more mature attitude toward religious beliefs. True belief lies neither on the plane of historical reality nor on the plane of mythological reality but on a level which surpasses both. Actually it operates synergetically, drawing from both planes, taking advantage of the sensitivities involved at both levels. The need today is to understand each of these levels more fully, and espcially to understand the synergetic combination of both in the act of belief.

Television's second main effect—the shift of meanings in the products it advertises—has considerable significance for the Christian's sense of sacramentality. In Genesis God asked Adam to name the animals; in naming them, Adam gained not simply their control but their cooperation. The church's tradition of sacramentality has always emphasized man's relationship to the world about him in a spirit of cooperation rather than outright control. What television commercials have done is to suggest a style of cooperation to which Christians might well become sensitized. The cooperation dramatized in commercials gives the products a value and fascination almost distinct from what they do and how they act. The style of life which the commercials depict may be that of a glorified kitsch U.S.A.; nevertheless, it is a style that says something valid about the way in which men of a technological society relate to the proliferation of products created by that society.

What emerges from the commercials points in an important direction for Christian sacramentality: the need for consciousness—active awareness of man's relationship to the things he owns and uses. The sophistication of the commercials to this point suggests that in future years the techniques of persuasion will become even more subtle, exploring—and encouraging—even further levels of relationship between man and the commodities depicted in the commercials. Christian sacramentality must become wide enough and open enough to accept the new possibilities, but critical enough and discerning enough to sense the limitations implied in the new relationships.

The third effect of television—the tendency to expect what one knows beforehand—has solid repercussions for the Christian's hope in Christ's return. What effect is had upon the Christian's expectation of an uncertain future by his daily choices of television series based on the certitude of what to expect there? We can only really anticipate the expectable—the early Christians sensed this in their hopes of Christ's return; television has reinforced it. A sense of Christian hope—which such recent theologians as Moltmann have tried to explore—must take into account the nature of expectation and how thoroughly modeled on the past expectations tend to be. All the more so in a television culture, where the basis for expectations is not only thoroughly clear but thoroughly confirmed, week after week.

The final effect of television—its tendency to shape consciousness—demands the strongest form of reaction. The shaping of consciousness is best met with an awareness of that shaping process; the best reaction to ads is not to ignore them (how, anyway, can one ignore ads?) but to become aware of what they are doing, or trying to do, to the reader. Film discussions and film criticism are popular on many campuses and in many churches; it seems that an even greater necessity would be for television criticism—not on the basis of dramatic effectiveness or symbolic meaning (television has little to do with either of these) but on the basis of the kind of consciousness most shows tend to form—the image of man they present, the conception of good and evil they dramatize, the assumptions about human relations and motivations which they build upon.

The effects suggest some of the complexity and perhaps the fundamental inscrutibility of the television interface. Yet it may be that television contains some of the most critical suggestions for the developing sensibilities which will shape the man of the future and the church of the future. Time—and what Christians consciously make of the television interface—will tell.

12

A Cybernetic Consciousness?

FORECASTING THE COMPUTER INTERFACE

Someday—not too far from now—people will "ride" their personal computers with all the excitement that the motorcycle rider feels when he storms down the long tunnel of the night. We will, with computers, explore our mental world with something that shares, amplifies and defines our experience. In doing so, it will help us define ourselves as human personalities.

Don Fabun*

In the man-machine gestalt, men experience the extension of their muscles and hands in technological form. When it comes to the computer—and the computer interface—man is going to encounter a creature far more threatening, though capable of far greater service: a technologically fashioned brain.

The words come out a torrent in today's journalism: automation, computer, cybernetics, information retrieval, feedback—there is almost no escaping the glowering face of a new epoch, as it begins to dawn. Yet what can we expect in this epoch—will the computer continue the trends of the machine or will

---

* *The Dynamics of Change* (Englewood Cliffs, N.J.: Prentice-Hall, 1967),
Part 4, "Automation," p. 19.

it initiate a revolution of greater proportions than we can conceive? More probably the latter, Dr. Jerome Wiesner, dean of science at M.I.T., has written in the New York *Times:*

> The computer, with its promise of a million-fold increase in man's capacity to handle information, will undoubtedly have the most far-reaching social consequences of any contemporary technical development. The potential for good in the computer, and the danger inherent in its misuse, exceed our ability to imagine. . . .

Whereas the previous chapters have dealt with existing environments and might be considered speculation on the present, any serious attention to the significance of computers for man falls into a different category: conjecture. We know something of the way in which computers work, and we have vague ideas of their possibilities for the future, but in terms both of their design and of the uses to which they might be put, computers are still infants—growing rapidly but more dependent on us than upon themselves for their growth and direction. Clearly, this will not always be the case.

As technology progresses, each important step involves a new mode of thinking to relate to the actuality of the new environment it creates. The steam engine not only revolutionized the design of other machines; it forced men to think about machines as ways of getting more from less—more energy from less effort, more work from less work. Previously, machines had been considered mechanisms that guaranteed greater accuracy and precision but not necessarily a proportion between less effort and more work. The leap in thought demanded by the computer is far greater than that involved with the steam engine. The computer's real significance does not lie in the "thinking power" of a little black box—or even in the new ability to process information as easily as we can process wool. Computers evolved from and lead toward a whole new conception of information: an awareness of information as a statistical quantity, the particular choice of a system in which a number of other choices are available. There is information in the flick of a light switch; in the feedback loop of a steam engine; in the homeostatic process of an oak leaf, determining how much chlorophyll it must produce. The computer is a machine by which all forms of information can be processed and manipulated: cybernetics is the science of information—its measurement, transmission, and control.

Norbert Wiener, one of the major pioneers in the development of the computer, and the man who coined the word "cybernetics," drew the term from *kybernetes,* a Greek word meaning "steersman." "The steering engines of a ship," he wrote, "are indeed one of the earliest and best developed forms of feedback mechanism." The feedback loop is a fundamental feature of all cybernetic systems, whether a computer or a nervous system. As information is relayed, say, to the brain, the brain organizes the information to determine its response; if a driver sees a stalled car ahead, his brain relays the information back to his hands and feet: slow down and prepare to swerve around it. Feedback involves input, the organization of information (both input and previous information), and output.

The importance of cybernetics is that it serves as the basis for locating a language common to men and machines—a language capable of relating information as we know it to the computer. Computers operate in one of two possible ways: analogically or digitally. Analog computers treat information in terms of likenesses—generally through measurements. A slide rule operates analogically, as does the face of a clock. Digital computers, on the other hand, treat information in a completely additive way: they count. Most of the large computers are digital; their accuracy and capacities offer greater advantages at present than the analog computer.

So far, this all sounds very technical, but the implications of such a new technical device as the computer, and of cybernetics as the science of information, promise to be profound, reaching into the recesses of human life and consciousness. Indeed, the computer and its method of handling information will change society by changing the ways we *think* about society, and how we look upon our roles and relationships in it.

No doubt the most disturbing threat of the computer for many people is its capacity to free almost all of us from work. The possibilities of automation—despite the millions of workers it has replaced—have only been glimpsed. Within a century, work as we know it may no longer exist; "jobs" will have been replaced by the periodic task of keeping information flowing into the network of automated devices which will surround us. Much of our education, our knowledge, our experience, will come from the "little black box" which may serve as a separate sense, a wholly new form of contact with the outer environment. As Don Fabun said in the opening quotation, "We will, with computers, explore our mental world with something that shares, amplifies and defines our experience." The man-computer interface will not only free us from work; it will give us the option of freeing us from ourselves or at least the part of ourselves that is locked in by the inability to make knowledge as real and structured a form of the person as his blood cells or nervous system.

For computers will not simply force upon us the need to find an alternative to work; they will offer us that alternative. New ways of registering knowledge, an unbelievably enlarged capacity for information, new possibilities of communication—

the computer's potential for a leisure-stricken society is even more phenomenal than its creation of such a world. Yet it is possible, even likely, that men will be hesitant and fearful about the computer, that the radically ambivalent reactions noticeable in man's response to many contemporary environments will be all the more apparent in the final age of the computer.

Man's disoriented, bewildered reaction to a world built on leisure rather than on work will no doubt be a major effect of the computer. The Protestant work ethic, which helped develop technology and a free enterprise system, will become a scab on the social organism rather than its soul. An education preparing young people for "jobs" will become a laughable anachronism; as McLuhan says, "We are suddenly threatened with a liberation that taxes our inner resources of self-employment and imaginative participation in society." The meaningful and creative use of time—not simply a vacant "filling" of time—will become a major challenge not only to the free growth of personalities but to a society more susceptible to manipulation than any previous society.

The challenge of leisure may be the most obvious effect of the computer, but it is hardly the most ominous. As the conversation between man and computer grows, and as a wider number of people learn the languages whereby they can communicate with computers, they will increasingly think in terms of these languages. As mentioned earlier, computers are capable of two types of thought; analogical and digital. Both of these are rigidly mathematical, purely "rational." A computer might scan the features of a sea and the features of a girl's eyes and yield some slight information on the resemblance present—but it would hardly contain the connotations or richness of the poet's observation that "her eyes shone light and deep as the sea." As computational thought becomes increasingly prevalent and necessary, the noncomputational—human and never wholly rational—may become less important, not only in major decisions but in the steady trends of daily consciousness.

A fascinating glimpse of "computational man" is afforded in the character of Spock on NBC's *Star Trek*. Spock is utterly intelligent and utterly rational. He exhibits no fear, no emotion, no enthusiasm, only a staggering memory and ruthless, unhampered logic. Even the quirks of literary characters of highly refined intelligence like Sherlock Holmes cannot be detected in Spock; his race (the Vulcans) live and breed from the mind—in the pattern of their world, as one of the show's characters comments in one episode, "there is only black and white."

Black and white: the simple yes-no basis of the binary system, on which all computers run. Spock may be an overdrawn caricature of the men who will converse as frequently with their computers as with other men, but many of the characteristics will hold true: a dependence on logic over sensibility; a tendency to perceive information through a mathematical visor; a preference for precision over nuance, measurement over imagination. It is interesting that *Star Trek*, while cast in the distant future, is still wed to a contemporary outlook of man: Spock's intelligence and logic can locate the flaw in an opponent, but it often takes the irrationality and feelings of Captain Kirk to land the fatal blow. In a sense the show is a saga of man triumphing over the computer, using both his own irrationality and the thought processes of the computer as weapons. Perhaps in forty years the *Star Trek* of that era will depict man conquering the computer with only computational thought as his resource.

Closely related to the second problem—the tendency of men to think computationally—is a third. What effect will our new concept of information have on the way in which people know? In other words, in a world of immediately accessible information, what will become of knowledge—and of insight, the ratios of knowledge created by the personal mind? The repercussions here are strongest for art and religion, in which insight—the inescapably personal aspect of knowledge—is fundamental. Will computational man be capable of insight, or will insight be capable of enabling men to distinguish between computational and noncomputational thought, even as they distinguish between reality and fantasy?

The fourth repercussion of the computer has already been felt to some extent: the omniscience of information leading to a loss of individual privacy and autonomy, and the changed nature of management and human relations.

The U.S. government, in establishing a large computer with mammoth memory banks and links with other computers, claims any other method for handling income taxes and other government functions such as draft classification would be hopelessly obsolete. Perhaps so. But such a national "baby-sitter" could well have repercussions on individuals unimagined by its designers or even the computer itself. Already large organizations that depend heavily on computers for testing job applicants have discovered that such a method tends to have a demoralizing effect on the men. And not simply because the applications are badly programmed (they usually are): people like to feel that their individuality depends upon things which cannot adequately go into a computer. "Do not fold, bend, or mutilate" is less a protest of becoming a punchcard in a huge processing machine than it is a clamor for recognition of the importance of what can't go on the punchcard.

It would be foolish, of course, to think that the far-flung impact of computers upon society can yield only these four effects. However, in terms of the response of Christians to the computer interface, these four effects suggest at least a good beginning.

For as with the television interface, man's confrontation with the computer is initiating new patterns of perception, rerouting modes of thought, shifting the scope and origins of power. Any attempt to get at its significance and implications for Christianity can at best be only suggestive.

As Norbert Wiener has noted in his remarkable *God and Golem, Inc.,* the computer does—or soon may—raise specifically theological questions of grave significance. One problem, which we accept more increasingly, is that of magic and miracle: they seem to be no longer the domain of God and his saints. As Wiener notes, had some inventive genius suggested or even built a computer three centuries ago, he—and his machine—might very well have been destroyed and "exorcised" in one angry impulse by the Inquisition. We have accepted, since then, the power which lies in man's domain, a power distinct from earlier forms of "magic" only because we now know why and how it works.

Two much grittier problems face theology as a result of the computer, however: our image of God as creator and our understanding of the nature of man.

God, we know, created man in his own image and likeness. But what if man is able to create machines in his own image and likeness—which not only duplicate what man can do but duplicate themselves as well? What happens to the image of God as creator in a world in which man is surrounded by evidence of his own creative genius, when he himself has spawned a race of beings who in turn must look to him as God?

The second problem seems even knottier for theology, for it touches on the uniqueness, indeed the spiritual nature, of man. Wiener discusses the problem briefly in *God and Golem, Inc.;* a much more elaborate treatment can be found in Mortimer Adler's *The Difference of Man and the Difference It Makes.*

Suppose, hypothesizes Adler, the computer can duplicate the major processes of human thought; that is, suppose it becomes possible to carry on a discussion with a computer behind a screen, not knowing whether it is a computer or a man—and after a long conversation thinking it is a man. Adler claims that at this point we will know man has nothing which distinguishes him substantially from the machine—no soul, no immortality. Adler's conclusion may seem abrupt and final, but the careful, structured logic of his treatment suggests that the computer may, after all, tell us more about the nature of man than many would like to admit.

The two theological problems are, of course, interrelated, and they lead to a third: the moral question of man's relationship with the computer. If men begin relating to the computers with the frequency and the seriousness with which they relate to one another, what moral standards should guide these relationships, if any? "Render unto man the things that are man's and unto the computer the things which are the computer's," suggests Wiener. Yet what belongs to which—and who finally is to make the key decisions, man or the computer? One of the greatest threats of the computer may lie here, in the area of major decision-making, where the temptation is strong to let the computer determine patterns and outcomes. The computer, after all, has no conscience.

These three problems are mentioned only as larger theological problems which may well evolve with the science of cybernetics. The four problems mentioned earlier have their repercussions for Christianity as well.

The first problem, leisure, has already received wide acknowledgment and treatment. The specter of a world in which man spends his time, discovers his identity, and locates sources for pride and confidence in himself through leisure and not work does have a challenging look about it. To suggest that the church should slough off its work ethic and construct an ethic of leisure and freedom as a response, however, would be both unrealistic and useless. The Protestant work ethic grew out of a period during which people acted from religious (at least religious in origin) motives. A major revolution such as Luther began could stimulate an ethos in which work and the individual struggling in the world would characterize the beliefs of generations. But the church no longer has this power. Fresh moral alternatives—in, for example, sex—are not pioneered as much by the church as by the media. The church, in fact, is fast losing its identity as a repository for moral standards.

Then how is the Christian community to respond to the crises imminent in a society sustained on a guaranteed annual income and committed primarily to leisure and not work? Leisure is, interestingly, one of the few possibilities open to man and not to the machine. A computer cannot "play" (or at least if it does, cannot distinguish this from work); sex is impossible for even the largest IBM models; what leisure will mean to man will give a meaning to man—it will give him that crucial distance he needs in an age of the man-computer interface. It is not simply a question of locating *individual* identity in an age of the computer; it is likewise a question of locating *human* identity. And just as the computer will offer new, unimaginable possibilities in knowing and thinking, man will have leisure time —and other people—to bolster his awareness of what it means to be human. It may be that the image of the hippie—or even closer, of a hip-quixotic character like Murray Burns in *A Thousand Clowns*—will come to characterize the society of a computerized world: people who are capable of expanding their minds through the computer, but likewise of enjoying life and enjoying each other.

If the Christian community orients itself in the coming decades to the possibilities of the human, considering the Incarnation rather than the disembodied Divine as its model, it may very well play an immense role in preparing men to live as men with machines that might otherwise threaten and conceivably shatter their identity. Today it is sometimes difficult to distinguish the work of an inner city church from highly sensitive social work; in the future—if the Christian community is to continue—it may well be difficult to distinguish its work from that of the artist, who will likewise be attempting to sensitize people to their own human capacities, the richness possible in awareness, vitality, sex.

If the church of the future takes the direction of the artist, the other repercussions of the computer mentioned earlier might well be avoided. Computational thought, with its powerful tendency to plunge man into a yes-no universe, would coexist with a far richer, more sensitive range of perceptions and thought patterns. Already films have sensitized us to the expressive meaning of a human face; radio and other sound media have enabled us to hear as never before. If the Christian community can use these media to awaken men to the miracle of their own lives rather than diminishing and forfeiting this miracle, the threat of computational thought, or even the threat of information's destroying insight, then no longer becomes a threat but a further possibility for man.

Likewise with the fourth effect of the computer, the breakdown of individuality and privacy. The IBM cards will accumulate; people will depend upon them as never before—for everything from finding a mate to determining where the fishing is best at a certain time of year. Again, what matters most is not that computational features of men are going down on IBM cards but that people everywhere acknowledge how much of themselves *can't* go on an IBM card. Such an acknowledgment can only come as a result of enlightened sensitivity: to the world, to people, and above all, to oneself.

The church of the future—if it is to *be* the church of the future—should exist, as did the church in the past, to save people. But not to save them for another world, or even for the "work" of building this world into some kind of utopia. No, it will save them as always not from themselves but for themselves—for the possibilities latent in their humanity, in their love and sensitivity to one another and to themselves.

13

The Environmental Christian

SKETCHINGS FOR THE CHURCH OF THE FUTURE

> The human being is engaged, throughout his life span, in an unceasing struggle to differentiate himself increasingly fully, not only from his human, but also from his non-human environment, while developing, in proportion as he succeeds in this differentiation, an increasingly meaningful related-ness with the latter environment as well as with his fellow human being.
>
> Harold Searles*

Man, these chapters have said, does not live either by bread or by the Word of God alone, but also by the airplanes, telephones, automatic dishwashers, and television sets that surround and support him. Environments need, as never before, to be understood; not only in the ways they affect our daily patterns of work and play, but the deeper patterns of perceptual orientation, psychological need, and capacities for freedom, thought, and imagination.

The confrontation between Christianity and the technological interface is therefore imperative, yet difficult. As this chapter

* *The Nonhuman Environment* (New York: International Universities Press, Inc., 1960), p. 30.

will show, Christianity is itself a complex of profound interfaces —between God and man in Jesus Christ; between Christ and the world in the church; between men and the earth in the sacraments. Yet these interfaces, and our understanding of them, grew out of a period in which the model of interface was natural —the simple relatedness of men in human communities, of men to the earth that they sowed and harvested, an earth they knew. Technological interfaces, by imposing on man's consciousness the reflection of his own efforts and awareness, drastically alter the nature and dynamics of interface.

Four major periods of interface relationships can be seen in human history. Each period suggests a distinct mode of awareness of the environment, and precise ways in which the environmental interface occurred and affected men. The first of these, the primeval interface, involved a subordination of men to natural processes. Nature held the mystery and power of a god; it could be tampered with only at great risk, or for specifically religious or survival reasons. Rather than make the environment reflect the shape of human life—as we attempt today—primeval man attempted to make life reflect the environment. Studies of early rituals, such as Theodor Gaster's *Thespis,* show how fertility and harvest rites represented an attempt to ritualize change in the environment, so as to enable men to participate in the processes of nature and thereby be enriched spiritually and physically.

The next period of interface grew with the early civilizations and especially the cities: Babylonia, Egypt, Greece, Rome. Here the early interface gave way to an attempt by men to disengage themselves from their natural environment—whether by their constructions of new environments, by thought which centered on man and not man-in-this-world, or by a process of education and development which emphasized man's distinctness from his environment, if not yet his ability to shape and control it. This was the period of anthropomorphism: of morality and law, of new cultures burgeoning and flourishing, of Christianity's origins and early development.

The anthropormorphic period viewed the universe as a backdrop for human struggles and human salvation. Temporal categories, developed to the scale of an individual's or a nation's history, were more meaningful and more prominent in consciousness than spatial—or directly environmental—categories. The term "world" meant primarily not an enormous scope of space and natural environments but a complex of the social and cultural contexts which men had created; it was an interpersonal, not specifically environmental, term.

Christianity grew out of this period and contributed to as much as it drew from the anthropomorphic view of existence. The belief that God had taken on the identity of a man could probably only have originated in such a period—and of course it spurred the direction of the period as well. Environments meant little, directly or indirectly, for the early Christians: their belief centered in human relationships and the conviction that God had made himself present at the center of these relationships, in his Son become man.

The next period of interface began roughly through the tenth and eleventh centuries; its growth has been chronicled brilliantly by Lynn White, Jr., in *Medieval Technology and Social Change*. Through innovations as seemingly simple yet as radical as the stirrup and the horse plow, medieval man slowly came to sense the capacities for his power over the environment. "By the mid-thirteenth century," White says, "a considerable group of active minds, stimulated not only by the technological successes of recent generations but also led on by the will-o'-the-wisp of perpetual motion, were beginning to generalize the concept of mechanical power. They were coming to think of the cosmos as a vast reservoir of energies to be tapped and used according to human intentions. They were power conscious to the point of fantasy."* But it was these fantasies which created postmedieval Europe, which unleashed the genius of a Galileo, a Bacon, a Newton. The belief that the world could be made to work for man created a new era in the history of interface, an era in which men attempted to control their environment, not simply let it control them.

The era has lasted into the twentieth century and has dissipated gradually with the twin realization that man can do more than control his environment—he can create it—and that environments need not be spatial or totally surrounding. The major difference in the new era lies in the effects of the new environment upon him. The anthropomorphic spirit, still pronounced throughout the third era, is disappearing; man is returning to a state of consciousness in which he views himself as part of the environment, inseparable from it. The difference between the first and present periods, however, is a critical one. For primeval man, the environment itself contained the power, and that power reflected God; all the feedback man received from the world around him prompted a religious response. Today the environment reflects man; he is surrounded, like a pampered child under a Christmas tree, by his own objects, reflections of his own desires and whims. The power, he knows uneasily, is his, and the absolutes that guided earlier man are gone.

The contemporary era gives man an image of himself as part of a larger whole, but a whole which he can create, change, or destroy. He is conscious of his environment more than men have been since primeval times; yet that consciousness has the effect, very often, of increasing his uneasiness. Christianity, such

* London: Oxford University Press, 1967, pp. 133–34.

a profound spiritual and moral force in previous eras of interface, seems too entrenched in an anthropomorphic view of the world to relate to a radically different interface situation. Its interfaces emphasize man and God, man and man, man and himself; they will not support a vision large enough to include nuclear weapons or the automobile, television commercials or mass magazines. Consequently the greatest challenge facing Christianity today lies in exploring its possibilities for a world of technological interfaces, breaking away from its anthropomorphic basis and redefining it in terms of a new interface situation.

Such a challenge cannot be handled simply on the level of a Christian political theory or a moral attitude toward appliances, modern cities, and the media. Even a future-oriented image of man, committed to Teilhard's "building the earth," fails to grasp the broad implications of a radical shift in the interface experience—a shift that demands Christian self-understanding through these interfaces.

Two steps are required in such a broad rescaling of the vision of Christianity: a deepened understanding of our contemporary interface situation and an attempt at every level of Christian consciousness to conceive Christian categories in terms of the new interfaces.

The remainder of this chapter will be an attempt to sketch in quick, suggestive lines some of the dimensions of a Christian community oriented on the basis of the contemporary interface situation. Already the previous chapters have probed some of the consequences of today's interfaces for the church. The interface situations described in those chapters will, hopefully, indicate the nature of today's environment. Now we will attempt a vision of the whole: Christianity and the various levels of Christian consciousness, as they might exist in a total response to the contemporary world.

Several assumptions underlie this approach, which should be noted here. The term "church" will be used frequently, not necessarily as meaning a continuation of present church institutions—which may or may not be capable of the revolutionary changes required by the present and coming decades—but as the viable Christian community, capable of meeting the present in all its implications. We will concentrate, likewise, on certain key aspects of the future church, emphasizing its inherent structures rather than its dynamics—which are so conditioned by the styles and demands of the moment that they cannot be easily pinpointed. Another premise, perhaps the most important one: the great task of an interface-conscious church in the future will be to enable the self-actualization of men through their interfaces. Hopefully a viable church, which sides today with the social worker, will in the not too distant future side with the artist and poet in keeping alive the wellsprings of the human; keeping man aware of his emotional and spiritual resources and the range of his possibilities as a human being.

For finally the great threat of a technological environment—and moreso of the approaching cybernetic environment—is its reduction of the human to a scale accessible to the machines men have built for themselves. The "paper people" who occupy the vast governmental, industrial, and educational bureaucracies represent one of the most lurid consequences of the new interface. In alliance with the computer, they prefigure a style of life grimly reminiscent of Orwell's *1984*, a style which not only encourages uniformity in thought and life but imposes dehumanized standards for that uniformity. Thanks to the new interface, evil has found a new definition: any systematic, organized attempt to reduce the scale and possibilities of human life. In an anthropomorphic age evil sprang from human action or omission; today it can spring from the environmental interface itself, unless there is great sensitivity and resistance. The church, with its belief in God's giving man a fullness of life, may be the major safeguard of the human in a thoroughly technologized and computerized environment.

The implications of the new interface situation for Christianity will be discussed in five areas: the church and the nature and structure of its beliefs; morality; religious education; liturgy; and the challenges posed to Christian theology. This approach, hopefully, cuts across the major layers of consciousness and decisive action of the Christian. First, for a look at the implications for the church and its beliefs.

In previous interface eras the church depended on its own environment, what Bonhoeffer calls somewhat derogatorily a "religious" environment. In many ways a hangover from the primeval interface, the religious environment kept man conscious of his own limitations and needs: God became very often an "answer," or a Savior; he was present at the other side of death, in the mystery and terror of an unexplained universe, in man's moral shortcomings. The church depended on the religious environment because it was strong enough to prompt deep beliefs, insure a moral conscience, weld the Christian community. But as Bonhoeffer has noted, the age of religion is past; its premises have been undercut by science and a new awareness of human life and human potential. Perhaps even more important, God seems unnecessary in an environment which reflects man and man's power.

"Secular theology," celebrated by such writers as Harvey Cox and J. A. T. Robinson, has signified one attempt to define the church in an age in which it can no longer depend on a religious environment. Yet the definition has inevitably lacked the church's most substantial direction: its clarification of the human, spiritual meaning of the contemporary interface. Rather than create an environment, the church should illuminate environments. Its history and its sensitivity to freedom, conscience, and the range of human alternatives almost demand that it become the antienvironment of a technological age. That is, it should sort out what is constructive and what is destructive in the new interfaces—what creates and what subverts the human. No one should be more aware of the principle and presence of radical ambivalence in a technological world than the church, whose responsibility lies largely in awakening men to the great dangers and the great potentials in the new interfaces.

How? On all the levels of Christian life and consciousness, the possibilities are immense. In the area of beliefs, for example, the church should at least become aware of the alternatives possible in its doctrines. Immediately to replace doctrine with what McLuhan calls probes would be foolish, and perhaps suicidal; but this does not mean discarding the possibility that most doctrines may eventually have to give way to probes. Teilhard's conception of Christianity, for example, with its dynamic thrust and sense of an evolving Christ, should not replace traditional doctrines of time, Christ, and redemption as a new doctrine so much as coexist with it, an alternative vision.

The understanding of interface likewise illuminates many traditional doctrines. Interfaces are potent and synergetic; they create effects which could never be deduced from a separate understanding of the two forces which create the interface. Christian belief is rooted in interface: between God and man throughout the Old Testament, between God and man in Christ's Incarnation, between Christ and world in the church. Traditionally the Incarnation has been viewed as redemptive, God's gift to man: a highly anthropomorphic vision of Christ. What if God were attempting, by incarnating his Son into a man, to communicate to men the ultimate significance and possibility of life in this world? What if Christ's early life as a carpenter were not simply a preparation for his late life, but as important a reflection of his purpose on earth as his last few years? Understandably, the early Christians concentrated on Christ's public life in describing him; yet is that a reflection of God's purpose—or of the anthropomorphic period in which the early Christians wrote?

The church itself can be understood afresh when seen as interface. Interfaces change; as the environments become more sophisticated, yielding more power or more information, our involvement in them changes, our need for them becomes more or less pronounced. As interface between Christ and the world, the church is capable of keeping the most vital aspects of the world's movement in touch with God's action. The true Christian community might be defined as the one in which the interface is alive and vital; not sapped by the weight of its own history, a monument to the past rather than a reverberation of the present. If the interface between God and the world is real, claim the presence of Christian community. A poverty march or a peace rally might well concentrate and dramatize God's activity better than the large structures which people attend on Sunday, where the world and God never really meet synergetically.

Secondly, Christian morality likewise can reflect the potential of Christianity in the new world of interfaces. Several previous chapters have treated some of the moral questions raised by contemporary environments: freedom tends to take on a spatial, rather than an interpersonal, orientation; leisure is becoming a precondition for moral thought, just as work has been for so long. Rather than concentrate on particular aspects of the new environment, the comments here will attempt to circumscribe the scope of morality for a Christian conscious of the new interfaces.

The major effort for a moral awareness in the present age of interface is to move from a three-sided conception of the moral world to a foursided one; that is, from a moral awareness that embraces only man, other men, and God to one which embraces man, other men, environments, and God. Situation ethics, one of the major trends in moral thought within this century, has emphasized the significance of environment; however, it has generally referred more to interpersonal and emotional environments than physical or technological ones. That the car has changed premarital sexual patterns does not affect the inherent moral standards of sexuality—or does it? The route many moral theologians have taken is to acknowledge, long after the car has affected these patterns and once the patterns have become painfully evident, that earlier sexual moralities were too formalized, too inhibited. Instead of looking to the environments, they look to the human response. Situation ethics is indeed necessary today, but the situations must be defined in terms that embrace the total new environments, not only the people involved.

The problem comes into sharp focus with nuclear weaponry. Can it be inherently immoral for man to create something? This is not an attempt to answer the question here, only to show how it should be posed. Nuclear weaponry, with its capacity for total, indiscriminate, and uncontrollable annihilation of an area, is an evil in its very existence. To approach the question of the hydrogen bomb on traditional moral grounds is to miss the only basis on which it can be understood aright: environmental interface as a moral concern.

Perhaps nowhere in Christian consciousness will the principle of radical ambivalence apply so thoroughly as in morality. There is a classic ethical principle, reaching back to Thomas Aquinas, that says any moral choice will have both a positive and a negative effect. The great moral choices—very often social—of a technological era tend to widen these effects, making the discrepancy far more pronounced than before. The choice, for example, to move from the present economic system to one with a satisfactory guaranteed annual income would have powerful repercussions in resolving poverty, but at the same time in decreasing the work force and changing the mentality toward personal autonomy in the country. Whichever choice is made, the choice eventually will have to be made, with the consequences equally severe on both sides.

As a result of radical ambivalence in moral choices, it is becoming more important that the consequences of each alternative be anticipated and coped with, both immediately and eventually. A responsibility to the future, not simply through vague efforts at planning a self-scaled utopia but through a foresight of the outflowing alternatives from important moral choices, must become a key factor in the moral conscience of the church. Deciding for "now" is not enough and will have grave repercussions if it is thought to be enough; both effects must be taken into consideration, and Christians must think out ways in which they can deal with the implications of the negative effects, even as they pursue the possibilities unleashed by the positive effects.

The third area in which Christianity must be understood through the new interfaces is the church's task of enabling Christians to actualize themselves, to discover their identities, their possibilities, their alternatives. This process of development in self-awareness has its main predecessor in religious education —although in the church sensitized to interface, the actual efforts in this area will differ enormously from what transpired in religious education in the past.

Christian education in the future will concentrate on the individual and the potentialities he can reach in freedom, insight, and self-awareness. The decision to remain a Christian or not will not be forced upon him; nor will that decision be the purpose of such education—simply the ability of the individual to come to that decision. In the past, religious education has concentrated on youth; in the future, both youth and adults should be included, for the process of self-actualization hardly ceases at adulthood.

The great danger confronting Christian education in the future will not be the continuation of unpalatable indoctrination—people, especially youth, can resist that—but the application of sophisticated techniques in the effort of "freeing" both youth and adults. Already such methods as group dynamics, carefully constructed audio-visual presentations, and modules predicting and demanding growth patterns have been developed, techniques which a teacher committed to a class but unsure of a method might leap after gratefully. Yet if the freedom and self-actualization of the person involved is the real purpose of Christian education, such techniques can only interfere. "Technique can never engender freedom," Ellul has stated, and the belief that it can—no matter what, no matter how "freeing" the technique—will only constrict the meaning of freedom for the teacher, and possibly for the students.

How then to pursue Christian education? Assuming the teacher-student structure will remain (which it well may not), the voice of authority should lie more among the students—especially among the youth—than in the teacher or the doctrines and institutions which the teacher represents. The process should be one of exploring the environments to which the students are exposed and the effect which these interfaces have upon the students. Self-awareness today can come about largely through an understanding of interfaces, both technological and interpersonal. The principal resources for Christian education in the future should not be the Bible and catechism, or even the reams of materials prepared today with contemporary art and catchy statements, but the environments which students confront daily: television, automobiles, advertising, all of them. This is not to neglect the heritage of Christianity, which likewise deserves attention, but to enable the students to find in that heritage meaningful alternatives, possibilities which appeal to them and relate those meaningful possibilities to the pressures and tensions of their lives.

The fourth area, liturgy, is of all the areas most acutely distant at present from the technological modalities of interface. Liturgy is communal worship, and it depends on a combination of rite and symbolism for its strength and meaning. Both rite and symbolism depend profoundly upon the interface sensitivity of their epoch; the imposition of rites and symbols from one interface epoch into another may give liturgy more majesty and mystery, but such imposition likewise reduces its meaningfulness, its touch.

Symbolism is a function of interface. That is, through the feedback man receives from an environment, he is able to construe meanings which clarify both his own condition and his relationship to the environment. The early Christian symbols reflect an environmental awareness in which the world was natural, a reflection and creation of God. Bread, wine, water, fish: these were immediate and natural, and they connoted to men the life-giving necessity they had for him. A symbol drawn from the world contained some of the mystery and gratuitousness of that world; bread and wine came from man's cooperation with nature, not his industrialized manipulation of it.

Ritual depends likewise on its interface epoch. Men have always lived by rhythms, originally the rhythms of days and nights and seasons. Rituals are ways of entering socially into these rhythms and responding to God in a way sensitive to man's dependence on the rhythms. Again, an environment which replaces night with thousands of neon lights and summer with air-conditioning units tends to break down the rhythms—though to create others. Admittedly, the newer rhythms tend to be mechanical, dominated more by the clock's measurement of time than nature's—and as a result, less human. The new rituals which have emerged to fill the void tend to be more specialized and thoroughly secular; the college or professional football game, the flower or yacht show—these have come to be for many the rituals by which time is marked and rhythms are felt.

In terms of Christian liturgy, the contemporary question of symbol and ritual is a profoundly difficult one to resolve, because the new environments reflect man rather than God. Natural symbols no longer connote a relationship with man's origins and his destiny; synthetic symbols connote man's powers and capacities, but not God's. Likewise, rituals have come to celebrate man's prowess—whether in sport or creativity—and not God's presence.

One of the keys to a new liturgy will be the exploration of a new symbolic understanding whereby the contemporary interfaces come to illuminate man in his relationship with other men, and finally with God. Some of the processes of this new symbolic understanding have been suggested in earlier chapters on movies, the automobile, and the machine. New perceptual capacities—such as the ability to grasp several adjacent images at once—and contemporary consciousness of environments and important events might provide some possibilities for experimentation in mixed media liturgy, concentrating on such themes as racial tension, Vietnam, and peace efforts as a means of touching conscience and thereby touching God. There is no question, however, that one of the most significant challenges to the church will be that of creating a liturgy with genuine roots in the contemporary interface situation.

The final area, theology, exists as the reflections of the Christian community upon the meaning of Christianity for its era. Here, rather than suggest definite directions, it might be best to prompt some of the questions which a theology of the future church might take up.

In the past, theologians have depended primarily on philosophy and earlier theology as major resources. A church directed from and to its environmental interfaces needs a theology which draws from the world about it for its major resources. Likewise, the anthropology to guide such a theology must necessarily break away from the anthropomorphic direction of earlier theological anthropology.

The problems facing theology in the future will be harsh ones. How conceive of the basic relationship patterns within Christianity: man and man, man and God, man and himself, in terms of environmental interface? By what standards can the radically ambivalent effects of a technological environment be judged? What are the moral implications of new technologies, especially the computer, and upon what moral basis should they be challenged? How describe—and more important, how enable—the process of self-actualization in a technological era? Many of the major categories in Christian thought, such as redemption, salvation, eternity, conversion, and sacrament, have been uprooted by the technological interface; how reconceive and redefine these concepts—or are they wholly meaningless? One of the major and growing questions today is to clarify the relationship between manipulation and freedom; how can freedom be pursued and attained in a culture in which the predominant forces tend to manipulate the individual to a point of no return?

Theology, no less than the state of Christianity which it articulates and prefigures, needs to take account of a world in which man is no longer what he has seemed for so many centuries. As the perceptible world changes, so does man change. We live today in a world in which the changes move at speeds that leave our minds spinning with the uncertainty of too-rapid motion. If Christianity is to speak throughout these changes, it must speak illuminated and not bewildered by them. The world belongs to him who can best see where it can go. Could that, even today, be Christ?

Bibliography

Rather than attempt to list the innumerable books about each of the interfaces covered in these chapters, this bibliography will suggest a few books which offer a wider perspective on the concept of interface.

R. Buckminster Fuller's writings, while complex and demanding, offer a heady vision of interface, seen from the viewpoint of universal systems and energy congregates. The best introduction to Fuller is either his *Education Automation* or Robert Marks' *The Dymaxion World of Buckminster Fuller* (both Southern Illinois University Press), which quotes Fuller extensively. Other valuable works are his autobiography, *Ideas and Integrities* (Prentice-Hall) and *No More Secondhand God* (Southern Illinois University Press).

The work of Marshall McLuhan is indispensable for a comprehension of interface. The two most valuable works are his early treatment of ads, *The Mechanical Bride* (Beacon Press), and *Understanding Media* (Mentor Books).

Several books which focus on technology and the relationship between men and the environments they have created deserve mention. *The Man-Made Object* (George Braziller), edited by Gyorgy Kepes, contains several valuable and provocative essays.

Arthur O. Lewis, Jr., has edited a paperback anthology that traces popular attitudes toward machines, *Of Men and Machines* (Dutton). The work of Lewis Mumford is widely known; two books especially, *Technics and Civilization* and *The Myth of the Machine,* focus on the technological interface, and *The City in History* remains one of the greatest treatments of the history of interface between men and their cities (all three published by Harcourt). Finally, a book which cannot be neglected for anyone seriously concerned about the nature of man's relationship with the environment he has constructed is Jacques Ellul's *The Technological Society* (transl. by John Wilkinson; Knopf), a masterful treatise and very probably a contemporary classic.

With all due deference to the preceding pages, books fail, finally, to communicate the dynamic character of interface. The best resources for a comprehension of interface are the interfaces themselves; the experiences from which we can reflect and judge their nature, proportions, significance. Two directions will be suggested here: aspects of the media which focus on the interface, consciously or not; and actual experiences which themselves are potent and therefore reliable measurements of interface.

It would be ideal if a box could accompany this book. It would contain an album of electronic music by someone like John Cage or David Rosenbloom. There would be a videotape episode of *Mission: Impossible,* and perhaps one of *Star Trek.* Included would be plenty of ads and commercials, for all sorts of products: good advertising, poor advertising—all of it either illuminating or confusing the interface expectations which people have for the products. Then there would be either a film or a videotape with sections out of various movies and television shows: sections in which guns or cars or elevators are shown, and how they figure into the dramatic sequences.

Alas, no box accompanies (or better, encloses) the book. However, the reader is encouraged to look and listen where he can: interfaces surround us and are a major theme of media and advertising.

There are, of course, interface experiences themselves. Someday drive from one location to another, then arrange to be driven the same route, and think about the difference. Try going an hour without using *any* electrical convenience—whether telephone or electric toothbrush. Then analyze very carefully the attitude such abnegation creates. Test-drive all kinds of cars. Travel on a "speaking" elevator. Visit Montreal's Expo. Spend an afternoon in the toy section of a big department store. Make a list of subjects you would like to discuss with a computer if you got the chance. Stand on an overpass above a jammed freeway at rush hour and take snapshots of the drivers. Interfaces can be highly revealing, often more revealing than anything that can be said or depicted about them.

Post-word

BY HERBERT W. RICHARDSON, St. Michael's College, Toronto

The message of William Kuhns' book is that our environment is always talking to us and trying to get us to talk with it. And further, whether we talk with it or whether we refuse, our environment still has an effect on us. There will be an interface, an interaction and communication between ourselves and our environment, even when we are unaware of it—even when we think that *only we* are talking, *only we* command.

Western scientific man characteristically assumes that the world is some dumb draftee, conscripted into his army. The rhetoric of Western science and theology is replete with metaphors that suggest the boot camp situation: man's responsibility is to *subjugate nature,* bring her under *control,* exercise *dominion* and *sovereignty* over her, make her *fulfill his hopes.*

Huston Smith tells a story contrasting the modern Western attitude with the attitude characteristic of the East. When Mount Everest was finally climbed for the first time, a newspaper headlined "HILARY CONQUERS EVEREST." "What an odd verb to use," remarked an Oriental. "Everest has not been conquered, but befriended." The trouble with Western man is that he doesn't feel the YIN. He doesn't feel the interface. He thinks

146

that life is YANG YANG YANG—not the dancing two, but the stomping one. He thinks life is some boy out marching, some bold, proud boy who imagines that the noise of his boots upon the road is *him*. He never realizes that the noise is also the hard resistance of the road and all its silence. He never realizes that everything is interface and interface is always *both*. Unless we become aware that everything is interface and interface is always *both*, we will fail to understand *how* we are in the world.

To think of nature and all her contents as "environment" means to know her as something in whom we live and move and have our being rather than as some thing over which we have an obligation to rule. The master/matter model has so oriented our reflections on nature and technology that—at least until the McLuhans and Fullers—our question has been, "Can man, through the power of technology, subjugate nature and put her down?" Or, conversely, "Will the technology man is using to be a master finally overwhelm man himself and make him a slave?"

The question of man, nature, and technology, if posed in terms of "Who will conquer whom?" will go on forever. The very way of asking it keeps the question forever unresolved. The master/matter approach falsifies the situation and extends it into an endless conflict. This is the secret of BATMAN VERSUS PENGUIN, archetypal modern melodrama. How odd it is that we realize the melodrama of sponsored serials, yet fail to recognize that we think of man versus nature in the same way. The master/matter model manufactures the melodrama of modern man.

Now if the world is not matter that we master, but our environment, our partner-in-life, then we need to hear her, talk with her and groove. We have to learn about the interface— for only as we know this can we respond with some appropriate action. So we must consider not only flowers, trees, dogs, sun, rain, stars, and all the living things that God has made, but we must also understand toys, cars, bombs, television, tablecloths, shopping centers, newspapers, clothes, and movies—all the living things that man has made. For even the things that man makes come alive and have a life of their own. They don't remain mere lifeless puppets that move only when we pull the strings. They are our living children, have some kind of soul. This truth is the story of Pinocchio and old Geppetto: the things we make come alive and we do not just move them, but they also move us.

Since mythological stories seem to have lost their power to communicate truth, let me cite an illustration from real life which makes clear the interface between man and his own creations. The story concerns my son John. It is his birthday and he has just received a two-wheeled bike. He tries to ride it, never having tried to ride a bike before. So his efforts, in the first minutes, are utterly without success. Half-angry, half-crying, he reappears. "Dad," he accuses, "Dad, I thought you told me that when I was six years old I could ride a bike."

Poor John. You missed the point. "When you are six years old you can ride a bike" is not like "When you are twenty-one you can buy a drink." It is not like this at all. Being six years old doesn't mean that you *know how* to ride a bike. It means, rather, that you are old enough to learn how to ride a bike. You can't just mount a bike and say "Gaddup, bike, I command you to go!" You can't ride *on a bike,* you have to ride *with a bike.* You lean with its sway, you follow its way. When you do this, it will sway with your lean, and follow your lead. For a bike is something alive, something you can't just *know* but have to feel. Once you have discovered this, then your bike will be your friend—not just "a thing," but YOUR THING.

A bike, then, is just like any other environment—always giving us feedback, offering a clue as to what we should do. A bike is an environment; so is a car—for both feed back information to help us know how to steer and reach. A toy is also an environment and so is a bomb and so is a building and so are newspapers and movies and television. For they all communicate with us, giving us information to read. All environments, all artifacts, are media—information producers and processors. And if we miss the information they are putting out, our whole experience of life will be wrong.

The reason modern Western man fails to pick up information from environments is that he is blind and deaf to the environments themselves. He is afflicted with a peculiar kind of myopia that focuses his attention on the foreground and makes the background invisible. Since environments are thought of as background, Western man altogether misses the information which environments are putting out. This is why his perceptions of the world are so startlingly askew: he only sees and hears half of it.

This peculiar deafness and blindness has become especially acute and debilitating since the seventeenth century. Among the doctors, the technical name for this disease is "empiricism." Empiricism is the state of mind wherein one notices—and hence supposes to be real—only the things that are standing in the foreground. These things, and only these, are supposed to "exist."

The word "exist" derives from the Latin *exsistere*, which means to stand out, surge out, or stick out from the background. Persons suffering from empiricism can only perceive and hear things that poke forward, strike their attention, stick out, talk loud, and make an "impression" on their senses. Things that stand back, are silent, and modestly don't push forward to make an impression are not perceived by people with empiricism.

They notice only what is first paying attention to them. For if something is not paying attention to them and impressing them, then sufferers from empiricism simply assume that it couldn't be real at all. The effect then is something like the effect of color blindness—except that it is *being blindness*.

The fallacy of empiricism is that in reality things don't have to be talking in order to speak. There is communication in the saying of a word and a communication in the not-saying of it. The not-saying of a word is really a saying by silence, a talking by not talking. But modern Western man wants things said by saying them rather than by not-saying them. He can't grasp a meaning unless it is mouthed, he can't believe a truth unless it is literal. He wants things spelled out in black and white.

The inability of our modern man to see the background and to hear what is said in its silence is paralleled by his inability to see the space that surrounds and flows about the particular objects which he does notice. He thinks that space is *empty*—that it is really nothing at all. For example, what does he see below:

(   )

He sees two parenthesis marks, with nothing in between. This explains why Western man finds Japanese painting so "unfinished" and Japanese painters so wasteful. The Japanese do not finish their paintings and do not use up all their paper. They leave most of it empty. But the Japanese painter, like the haiku poet, tells most of his message through silence, saying it by leaving it unsaid. His brushstrokes or his several words are only the few needed to allow the spaces and silences, pregnant with meaning, to speak for themselves. But Western man cannot see such spaces or hear such silences. He is suffering from empiricism.

In the same way, modern man also finds the time between events to be empty and devoid of meaning. Time when nothing is happening is, he supposes, absolutely nothing. For him, the temporally real consists quite simply of the particular events that happen in time. So when things are not happening ONERIGHT-AFTERTHEOTHER, he is either bored or nervous. He just must fill up all that empty time. If nothing is happening, he creates pseudo-events to fill up the background.

Strictly speaking, of course, the space in which objects swim and the time that flows around events need not be *back*ground; and strictly speaking, the things and events that exist in space and time need not be *fore*ground. For the Japanese, who outline not objects in space but spacial masses with the help of objects, space itself is much fuller, much heavier, and much more forward than it is for Western man. Hence, we see that the background and the foreground can be interchanged. You've seen the tricks psychologists use to prove this point. And because backgrounds and foregrounds are interchangeable, there can be a speech both in talking and in not-talking. Hence all things communicate with us in two fundamentally different ways— and this is why environments, without being obvious, can still shape our experience of the world.

Let us examine some ways in which environments do shape our experience of the world. Consider the bicycle once again. Now the first day John got his bicycle, and during all the days he was learning to ride it well, the bicycle was right *there*, very obvious, up front. It was all foreground. The only thing in the world was his bike. But as he learned to ride it, swinging with its sway until the swing became so natural it took no conscious effort at all, John gradually forgot the presence of his bike even while riding it. And as he became accustomed to the fun of "just riding"—until "just riding" became no particular fun at all—John no longer went out with riding as his object. He now went out only to ride *somewhere*. Then, while riding along, forgetful of the bike that he was riding, it was this somewhere that was in the front of his mind. John's bicycle had now become pure background to his experience. John's bicycle had become a camera that establishes certain limits within which he experienced everything else. And yet he was no longer aware of his bicycle even though it was creating the overall background and total orientation for his sensing and feeling and understanding of the world.

The fact that John was unaware that his moving bicycle was providing background information does not mean that the bicycle was not doing it. It does not mean that John was not getting information from his bike, learning something even while unaware that he was learning. His contact with the bike was changing his experience of the foreground, changing his impressions of particular things, changing his feelings about the weightiness, texture, and reality of space and time.

Edward Hall gives us another example of the way in which contact with a moving vehicle changes our experience of particular objects.* He contrasts an experience of an automobile drive through the deserts of New Mexico with a walk over the same terrain. At walking speeds, he recalls, even the nearsighted can see trees, shrubbery, leaves, grass, the surface of rocks and stones, grains of sand, ants beetles, caterpillars, and even gnats. But driving an automobile through the same area gives one a completely different picture. Not only is near-vision blurred by the speed of the automobile, but one's relation to the countryside is vastly altered.

* Edward Hall, *The Hidden Dimension* (New York: Doubleday, 1966), p. 165.

Hall shows that our experience of the world while riding in a vehicle affects our sense of space itself. The speed of our vehicle affects our sense of space itself. The speed of our vehicle seems to render the space through which we move less heavy, less resistant, less real. Space no longer seems to flow and coagulate around particular objects, making them stand out, giving them a unique individuality. When we are walking, on the other hand, space and time seem thicker and more real, becoming noticeable impediments to our progress. To encompass the particular objects is now experienced as more difficult and the pace of our movement is slow. The very slowness of our pace forces us to see the world in terms of many small particulars. Not only do we experience the world to be composed of a multitude of individual objects, but even our method of communicating and thinking is affected. When walking we tend to talk slowly, expansively, concretely, naming each thing seen, lingering over detail, and describing each item in an unhurried narrative story.

How different is the experience—and the narrative style—of the typical American, who seldom observes the world from the vantage point of walking. He has not seen a grain of sand—though he has seen a desert. He has not noticed a single gnat—though "insects" have hit against the front windshield of his car. And because this is how he experiences the world while driving through a desert, his description of the journey will be briefer, more abstract, less a narrative with novelistic character than a terse journalistic account.

All this suggests that the reason why Americans find the lenthy novel inadequate as a literary form, preferring, rather, the brevity and pace of the short story, is because their experience of the world presupposes the spatio-temporal feeling characteristic of the moving automobile. In sharp contrast, the lengthy narrative novels by Charles Dickens or Sir Walter Scott expressed the feelings of men who assumed the spatio-temporal experience of the world characteristic of walking was most adequate in gaining a proper understanding of reality. But to an American, the pace, the movement, the detail characteristic of these English novels seems so false to his experience, so contrived and artificial, that he can't understand how anyone has ever found them interesting and readable.

Notice, too, that interface with a moving vehicle also affects our sense of the distinctiveness, relatedness, and uniqueness of the objects we see.. When we *walk* along, because of the slow pace of our movement, we experience

TREE   SHRUB   GRASS   ANT   BEETLE   ROCK

But if were to traverse the same course while riding a bicycle, we would experience

TREE   SHRUB   GRASS   ANT   BEETLE   ROCK   FLY   SAND

Moreover, if we were to speed over the same road in an automobile, we would see

TREESHRUBGRASSANTBEETLEROCKFLYSANDMOSQUITOBIRDSTONE

The faster we are moving, the less distinctiveness and individuality objects seem to have. They seem now to be related to one another, perhaps even blending and fusing into a single dynamic process. Moreover, if—like John riding his bicycle—we forget the speed of our automobile, forget perhaps that it is *we* who are moving, then we experience the world outside the car to be in motion. It seems to be constantly changing, one thing blending into the next until there is one organic and dynamic whole. And as we come to experience the world more and more in terms of change—whether it be in full awareness of our motion or be a sense of change in the world itself—we also come to assume that change is a normal state of affairs and that reality is process.

To assume that change is normal is a very unusual idea indeed, although such a conviction is now deeply rooted in the mind of modern Western man. Most societies have assumed change to be abnormal; they have regarded it with fear and seen it as a threat to their lives. Most cultures have assumed that the normal state of affairs is permanence and stasis—so much so that they have identified God himself with immutability, unchangeability, and with solidity characteristic of rocks and mountains. How is the difference between our modern feeling and that of more traditional societies to be explained?

I suggest the difference between the traditional experience of change and the modern experience of change may be primarily a result of the technological interface. For whereas the traditional society assumed that experience of the world gained while walking was "normal," we assume that our experience of the world gained through rapid motion is "normal." It could be, therefore, that the question whether reality is change or the changeless is not so much a problem in metaphysics, as many philosophers have assumed, but rather a problem in technological interface.

We should keep in mind that the vogue of "process philosophies" and the popular belief in "progress" coincide exactly with the invention and widespread use of the automobile and the movie camera. This suggests that much of modern philosophy may simply be an offshoot—or perhaps an ideology—of the automobile. Of course, this may not be the case, but since no one has even considered the possibility, it does not seem perverse to suggest it as a hypothesis worthy of investigation.

Moreover, we should also consider whether the empiricistic event-orientation of modern man, his peculiar blindness to background space and time, and the vogue of empiricism (which justifies secularism) are not also the result of certain technological interfaces. If they were, then it would mean that those contemporary theologians who proclaim that Christianity is a historical "event-oriented" religion—elaborating the "Christ-event," the "speech-event," the "acts of God," and theology as the "recital of historical happenings"—are not so much discovering this insight in the Bible, but allowing the technological interface that breaks down our awareness of backgrounds and multiple-meanings to control their academic investigations.

I myself have no doubt that this is the case. And I have no doubt that the newer kinds of technology—especially television and certain types of consciousness-expanding chemicals—shall produce a different interface effect on us than the automobile did and hence cause us to read Scripture differently and develop new theologies. This is, of course, the thesis of Marshall Mc-Luhan—and it is the thesis of William Kuhns in the present book. I am happy to confess how much I have learned from them both.

Format by Katharine Sitterly
Set in Linotype Fairfield
Composed, printed and bound by The Haddon Craftsmen, Inc.
HARPER & ROW, PUBLISHERS, INCORPORATED